Hauntings and Poltergeists

A Ghost Hunter's Guide

by Loyd Auerbach

PROFESSOR PARANORMAL

Ronin Publishing

Berkeley, CA

Hauntings & Poltergeists

Copyright 2004 by Loyd Auerbach

ISBN: 1-57951-072-8

Published by

Ronin Publishing, Inc.

PO Box 22900

Oakland, CA 94609

www.roninpub.com

Production:

Editor:	Beverly Potter	docpotter.com
Cover Design:	Brian Groppe	briangroppe.com
Book Design:	Beverly Potter	
Layout	Brian McCracken	luminsa.com

Fonts:

Brutality, Jakob Fischer/PizzaDude, pizzadude.cjb.net

Gouty Old Style, URW Software

Nightmare, Astigmatic One Eye Foundy, astigmatic.com

Palatino, Apple Computer

Tussle, 2001 Iconian Fonts, iconian.com

Library of Congress Card Number: 2004096984

Distributed to the book trade by **Publishers Group West**

Printed in the United States by United Graphics

Dedication

To Mom & Dad with love,
as they reach their Golden Anniversary

Acknowledgments

First, I want to thank my wife, Julie, for her continual support of my writing process (and all the other weirdness in my life). Then, too, my friends and many colleagues who keep offering their support, kindness, friendship, and good humor.

Also, I need to acknowledge Robert L. Morris, who held the Koestler Chair of Parapsychology at the University of Edinburgh, and was an incredible influence in the field. Bob died suddenly, just as I was working on the final edits of this book. Bob had a multiple impact on me—on my knowledge and thinking processes, on my interest in magic and mentalism, and on my sense of humor. He was a great thinker and a very funny man.

Finally, let me acknowledge folks out there starting their own ghost hunting groups. I may seem a little hard on you, but that's only to encourage you to learn as much as you can do as to make a real impact on the lives of people around you—living and dead.

TABLE OF CONTENTS

Introduction 7

Parapsychology 10

Extra Sensory Perception 18

Psychokinesis 26

Survival 36

Beginnings 44

In the Lab 54

Apparitions 63

Apparitions and Psi 74

Hauntings 84

Hauntings and Psi 92

Poltergeists 102

Poltergeists and Psi 110

Controversy 119

Not Psi 125

The Case of Lois 134

The Sexorcists Case 143

Two Poltergeists 149

Weird Not Paranormal 157

Ghost Hunting Tips 164

Being Psychic 173

Developing Psi 181

Index 189

Author Bio 191

Ronin Books for Independnet Minds 192

INTRODUCTION

N YOUR HANDS IS A BOOK that provides the background that you need to understand the phenomena of apparitions, hauntings, and poltergeists, commonly called "ghosts".

This background is necessary for real investigations, and even more necessary if you wish to help people deal with such experiences. You will find discussions of different types of ghosts—what we designate apparitions, hauntings and poltergeists—and discussions of Parapsychology, the field of science that examines these phenomena.

Hauntings & Poltergeists gives you insight into what parapsychologists study, current findings, and why "proof" of ghosts and related phenomena has been so elusive—or simply so difficult to convince others. The necessity of understanding ESP and mind-over-matter abilities and experiences in trying to understand spirits, haunted places, and poltergeist outbreaks will be clear to you.

Hauntings & Poltergeists also provides insight into a few of my own cases. This is not just a book *about* ghosts. *Hauntings & Poltergeists* is for anyone interested in the paranormal generally, and particularly in psychic phenomena and abilities—which includes encounters with poltergeists, ghosts, and visitations in haunted houses. It is for those interested in life after death and a specific interest in the ghostly side of life.

Hauntings & Poltergeist provides you with a basis for understanding your own experiences with spirits and poltergeists. It is for anyone who is currently or wants to become a ghost hunter. People without awareness of the literature of parapsychology who read this book will learn that there are many other explanations for orbs, voices and energy fields detected and recorded, or for "evil spirits". Many books tell you they can sum up all you need to know to investigate haunted houses but sidestep discussion of psychic phenomena in life and lab. Like my other book, *Ghost Hunting,* this book educates and motivates new ghost-hunters (you) to become *investigators*, looking for what is *really* happening. It will excite you to know that there is so much more to learn and investigate.

Hauntings & Poltergeists is an introduction and overview. It is valuable for the true beginner and for the well-read. To be a paranormal investigator, you need the information in this book. If you are just an interested party, it will give you insight into the thought processes of professional paranormal field investigators.

If you are a true believer or a true disbeliever, you may not agree with everything in this book but I hope it will make you think. It is not meant as the final word on the subject since we are all still learning in parapsychology.

For the majority somewhere between those two ends of the belief spectrum, this book will also make you think, but will especially appeal to the sense of wonder in most of us. After all, isn't the possibility of greater human potential a wonderful idea?

1

PARAPSYCHOLOGY

HE FIELD OF PARAPSYCHOLOGY was born IN 1882, with the founding of the Society for Psychical Research. In the beginning, the field known as psychical research had a primary focus on psychic events that occur spontaneously in people's lives, including ghosts and hauntings.

In the early 20th Century, the emphasis shifted. Parapsychology, as the field was now called, turned toward controlled laboratory studies of psychic abilities and away from the investigation of cases of apparent survival of death. While the interest in spontaneous case investigations never ended, it waned more than a little. But well before century's end there was a resurgence of interest in psychic experiences in daily life and in field investigation.

Parapsychology is the study of psychic or *psi* phenomena (pronounced "sigh"), defined as exchanges of information between living things—mainly people— or between living things and the environment, as well as influences of living things on the environment that occur without the use of the "normal" senses and are not apparently explicable by the currently accepted physical laws of nature. Throughout this book the term *psi* is used interchangeably with "psychic." *Psi*, by the way, is the term chosen by parapsychologists to refer to these experiences because it is the 23rd letter of the Greek alphabet, noting an "unknown."

Parapsychology as a science is concerned with connections and consciousness—or mind. Parapsychologists study consciousness: Does the mind have channels of information flow other than the "normal" senses; can it can connect with the minds of others and reach out and affect the world directly; and can it survive the death of the body. Parapsychologists study consciousness in terms of connection, interconnectedness, and existence aside from the body, and ask if there's more to consciousness than many in mainstream science accept. The experiences they study are grouped into three main categories: receptive psi, expressive psi, and survival of physical death.

RECEPTIVE PSI

THE FIRST GROUP OF PHENOMENA, called *receptive psi*, is probably more familiar as ESP or extrasensory perception. In the 1980s, psychologist and psi researcher Keith Harary came up with a more descriptive term for ESP: *extended* sensory perception. Now, the phrase *anomalous cognition*—unexplained knowing—is used.

Included in this category are various abilities involving the transfer or communication of information. Such as information apparently shared between two or more minds, information drawn from objects and events, and information communicated through time, from the future or the past.

EXPRESSIVE PSI

THE SECOND GROUP OF INTERACTIONS is collectively referred to as *expressive psi*, or "mind over matter." The term that parapsychologists have applied to the wide range of effects and abilities in this category is *psychokinesis*, or more simply, PK. Here we are talking about true mind over matter—the ability of the mind to influence material objects or processes without the use of known physical forces.

SURVIVAL OF BODILY DEATH

OF CENTRAL IMPORTANCE TO HUMANITY SINCE THE DAWN of time is the concept of life after death or, as parapsychologists like to put it, the "survival of bodily death"—*Survival*, for short. This was the major area of investigation for the early psychical researchers. Experiences involving communication with a deceased person, recollections of a past life, or even personal experiences of dying and death—actually near-death— are studied under this category.

GHOSTS

WHILE IT MIGHT SEEM THAT SURVIVAL would be the main category to look at for ghostly encounters and hauntings, it's not. In reality, there are three basic categories into which "ghost" phenomena have been grouped: apparitions, hauntings, and poltergeists. The three are different conceptually, but events around each can appear similar and can even indicate unique combinations of phenomena. Interestingly, each can be connected to one of the main categories of parapsychology: hauntings to ESP, poltergeists to PK, and apparitions to

Survival. Before getting into the specifics of these three areas or the three types of ghosts, let me give you a quick defining overview.

A HAUNTING REFRAIN

THE EXISTENCE OF HAUNTINGS actually shows that we are all psychic receivers to some degree. Do you ever walk into a house and get a feel for the "vibes"—the house feels "good" or "bad"? Of course, the vibes you get could result from normal perceptions—the decor, for example, may be nice or a turnoff. Alternatively, you may also be psychically perceiving emotions and events embedded in the environment.

Hauntings are connected to locations, whether a building or a piece of land, and sometimes to objects such as furniture. People perceive a range of things in haunted places, from unusual emotions, to unexpected sounds and smells, to visuals of people walking about or doing some activity. The events or visuals happen over and over, like a recording stuck in one spot.

The best explanation parapsychologists have of hauntings is that somehow the local environment picks up information from people and events and records it. We living folks—and sometimes our pets—can pick up

Hauntings have nothing to do with appearance.

snippets of such recordings of past happenings. Think of a haunting as a loop of video or audio tape playing itself over and over for you to watch. Trying to interact with it would be akin to trying to interact with a show on your TV. You can turn the stress off or change the channel, but you wouldn't expect the actors to suddenly stop and talk directly to you. In other words, when you see a "ghost" in a haunting, you're psychically perceiving a kind of recording. Since you are receiving information, haunting encounters fall in the category of receptive psi.

PARANORMAL STRESS RELIEF VALVE

FROM A PARAPSYCHOLOGICAL PERSPECTIVE the term *poltergeist*, while it literally translates as "noisy ghost," has come to denote something altogether different. In poltergeist cases, physical effects are the central theme. Effects range from movements, levitations, and the appearance or disappearance of objects to unusual behavior of electrical appliances; from unexplained knockings to temperature changes—with all combinations possible. Rarely are ghostly figures or voices seen or heard, though they are not out of the question.

Parapsychologists explain poltergeist as a situation caused by the subconscious mind of a *living agent*, undergoing emotional and/or psychological stress. The agents are people who generally reside in the household and typically have limited means of dealing with the stress in a normal manner. So the subconscious takes advantage of the mind-over-matter ability we all have to blow off steam. Think of the poltergeist scenario as a sort of telekinetic temper tantrum. Since poltergeist events come from an effect of the mind, it in the expressive psi category.

HANGING AROUND AFTER DEATH

FINALLY, WE COME TO ACTUAL SPIRITS—apparitions of the dead. The concept of apparitions is truly related to Survival. An apparition is our personality—or spirit, soul, consciousness, mind, or whatever you prefer to call it—surviving the death of the body, and capable of *interaction* with the living and presumably with other apparitions.

The phenomenon of interaction separates an apparition from a haunting ghost. If a haunting is like a replay of videotape, an apparition is a video conference call. While speaking to the videotape brings no response, the conference call allows for two-way communication.

This category contains not just apparitions of the dead, by the way. There are thousands of reported cases of apparitions of the living. Even these experiences are indications of the survival of human consciousness beyond death of the body. More on this later.

SO, WHAT IS A GHOST?

THE TERM *GHOST* can mean many things to many people in different cultures and religions—and clearly to different film and TV producers. For the most part, the word has come to

mean something, or someone, that exists
without a body, yet can be perceived by us
living folks. The word is usually associated with a part of a
formerly living person or
animal—sometimes called spirit—
that still exists. However, *ghost* has
also been applied to disembodied beings
that were never alive, such as the demons
and angels found in some religions and
mythologies. In fact, more than a thousand years
ago—and still today in a few regions and in some
people's religious beliefs—many people around the
world believed that ghosts were evil entities that
pretended to be apparitions of loved ones who had
died. However, the evidence we have today is contrary to this belief. In this book the term *ghosts* will
be limited to its more common meaning of spirits of
the dead, or apparitions, and I'll use the terms
interchangeably.

WHY KNOWLEDGE OF PSI?

TRYING TO COMPREHEND and create models of what
ghosts, hauntings, and poltergeists are is futile without the framework of psi and parapsychology.

Hauntings rely on some non-normal perceptions
of information—in other words, ESP. Poltergeists don't
exist outside of the concept of PK. Both involve the
psychic abilities of the living. Apparitions, not having
a physical form, must communicate and interact with
the living using some kind of psychic process—ESP.
In those rare cases where apparitions can move
objects, they must be doing this by PK, by mind
over matter. After all, apparitions are of the mind.

So, understanding the psychic abilities of the living is essential to understanding how all this ghostly stuff works, and what to do about it. Now let's look at the three areas of parapsychological study, starting with receptive psi.

2

Extra Sensory Perception

XTRA-SENSORY PERCEPTION—popularly called ESP—abilities are among the most commonly reported, and likely the ones more commonly experienced. They are also the most commonly ignored. If you suddenly know something without any awareness of where that information came from, you may simply write it off as instinct, intuition, coincidence, or even something you'd forgotten you knew. By contrast, if you saw an object floating through the air or a person appearing or disappearing you're certainly likely to *notice* it, even though you may it write off as happening in your "imagination"

Extrasensory means "beyond the sensory." No sensory structure in the body has been identified to being able to physically picks up this kind of information, which means the abilities may not be sensory in the way we think of the senses. But it *is* perception. Information is processed by the brain-mind. How that information gets into the perceptual process is the mystery, since we know the limitations of our normal senses and most reported receptive psi experiences are beyond those limits. Parapsychologists believe that everyone has some degree of ESP or at least potential for ESP.

PERCEPTION

WE THINK OF PERCEPTION as being all about our five normal senses. However, perception is partly the receipt of information and partly information processing. But wait a minute—only five senses? Actually, experts argue about how many senses we really have. The sense of touch, for example, is often broken down into several senses: pressure sense, hot sense, cold sense, pain sense, texture sense, and so on. Different touch receptors are responsible for different kinds of touch perception. Similarly, the sense of taste can be broken into salty, sweet, sour, and more. Some put the number of senses at more than fifteen.

Even when we group touch and taste as single senses with what we consider our other "normal" senses of sight, hearing, and smell, there are still have more than five. ESP is not our "sixth sense."

There is also the sense of balance, for example. Inside the inner ear is a structure responsible for balance—sense of body-position. The information gathered by the inner ear is processed in the brain-mind, and perceived on both a conscious and unconscious level, much like our other senses.

So is ESP then the seventh sense? Maybe not. Many animals and possible some people have the ability to sense and perceive magnetic fields. In the mid-1990s, magnetic material was found in normal human brain tissue, providing a link between magnetic fields and the brain. It's been suggested that those who claim to see the human aura are actually sensing the magnetic field around people, which their perceptual processes translate the into a visual impression of color.

Perceptual processing can transform the input of our normal senses. Synesthesia is a condition in which an individual's sensory perceptions are mixed up. Colors can be tasted, music can be smelled, and smells can be seen—and other variations. This condition happens during some altered states of consciousness, such as those induced by LSD and "magic" mushrooms and by certain physical changes in the brain.

People often misinterpret the data from their senses. The perceptual process both screens out extraneous information and fills in some blanks. What the eye actually sees and what the brain tells us the eye sees may be quire different.

Perception is learned. We learn to see the world in a particular way, based upon our cultural background. The way we have learned to perceive things in one physical environment and culture may distort input that doesn't relate to that original environment. We expect things to behave in a certain way, and may unconsciously ignore happenings that don't fit what we expect as "normal."

Expectations can be superimposed over the way objects and events actually, objectively exist, often giving us a distorted perception. Past experience, current and past motives, the context of the event, or suggestion can set us up to perceive things in particular ways that may not actually reflect reality. We tend to perceive what we want and expect, especially when the event is of short duration and happens in an out-of-the-ordinary way.

There's a lot more to perception than what we receive through the normal senses. Parapsychological research suggests that some information coming into the brain-mind and included in the perceptual process may be from input other than what the senses provide

TELEPATHY

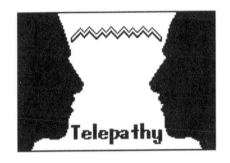

TELEPATHY is an awareness of information or emotions that exist in the mind of another. It is kind of "mind-to-mind" communication and not the stereotype of "reading" someone's mind. Transfer of information often occurs spontaneously, when you least expect it.

People seem to "broadcast" thoughts that others may pick up spontaneously. Think of all the chatter happening in your head—your internal running monologue. There's a lot there, and there's much more in your unconscious mind and in your memory underneath that chatter. When someone apparently picks up a thought from you, it's not that the person is *reading* your mind as much as *receiving* a broadcast signal. Rather than probing your mind, psychics tune in to your broadcast frequency.

Studies have also indicated that it is fairly simple to block anyone from receiving information from your mind, and to block your mind from receiving thoughts of others. You can stop transmissions from your mind to others by blanking your mind, or focusing on a single thought—like a song running through your mind over and over—or visualizing a force field or wall around your head. You can block out others thoughts from invading your mind by shifting your attention to something else or erecting a mental barrier to keep stray thoughts out.

CLAIRVOYANCE

THE FRENCH TERM, *Clairvoyance*, means "clear seeing" and refers to the receiving of information from objects or events at the *present* time without the use

of the "normal" senses or logically piecing things together from clues. The term literally refers to visual information, but parapsychologists include under this heading information that comes in as perceptions of sound, physical sensation and smells. Clairvoyance is believed to be the underlying process in remote viewing, psychometry and dowsing.

The late Mrs. Aiko Gibo, of Yokohama, Japan, did this drawing of an Australian aboriginal sacred site while 60 miles away."

Remote Viewing

You likely have seen or heard the term *remote viewing*. Remote viewing (also known as Remote Sensing) is the ability to perceive sounds, feelings, sensations, smells, or tastes that are not within the range of the senses. Today, most researchers use the terms *remote viewing* (RV) or *anomalous cognition* (AC).

Psychometry

Psychometry is the ability to "read" the history of an object or location, or gain information about the people associated with it. Some psychics say they receive information through the vibrations that an object, location of the field around it gives.

One theory is that all material objects actually can somehow record information in the electromagnetic field that surrounds matter or through some other means, and that some people are able to decode that information.

Psychometry is believed to be the underlying dynamic of *hauntings*, where an apparition is seen or heard or felt to perform the same acts over and over, like a replay of past events. You may enter a so-called "haunted house," pick up on the history of the location, and have your mind provide a replay of some of the events from that place's past.

One aspect of this model is that it posits a real physical explanation for this form of ESP, one that fits in and can be explained by the new quantum physics. Another explanation for psychometry is that the object merely acts as a focus for the psi abilities of the person doing the reading, enabling her to clairvoyantly locate appropriate information. This is the reason why psychics often request an item owned by a missing person before trying to locate that person. Tarot cards, crystal balls, and other such occult items often serve as a focal point for a psychic to tune in to something clairvoyantly.

DOWSING

DOWSING, ALSO KNOWN AS RADIESTHESIA, may be clairvoyance. A dowser may use a forked stick, a wire, or some other object to focus in on to locate water—sometimes called *water-witching*—oil, mineral deposits, even explosives. Dowsers were reportedly used by the First and Fifth Marine Corps Divisions in the Vietnam War to locate mines, booby-traps, and tunnels.

The author in Australia with psychics Aiko Gibo and Suzane Myles.

Whether this ability is related to clairvoyance, to some kind of magnetic sensing, or to something else has yet to be determined.

PRECOGNITION

PRECOGNITION IS THE ABILITY to receive information about objects or events that exist in some future time. Of all the psi abilities parapsychologists study, precognition has always held the most fascination for humanity.

We're constantly hearing or reading about some psychic making a new prediction, and at the same time can't help but wonder why those same psychics aren't doing things like making money at the racetrack. Of all the psi abilities, precognition has the most uncertainty associated with it, since we really don't know if information can cross time, or if the future is set enough for us to actually read what is going to happen.

RETROCOGNITION

RETROCOGNITION IS THE AWARENESS of objects and events that existed in the past. The past, unlike the future, *has* already happened, so many people find this ability somewhat easier to understand. In fact, this proposed psi talent has been suggested as an alterna-  tive explanation to psychometry, and therefore hauntings, in the sense that instead of reading the history of an object or location from some energy field, the person receiving the information is simply using that object or location as a focal point to look into the past.

3

PSYCHOKINESIS

 AN YOU MOVE MATTER with your mind? Of course you can. You're doing it right now—your mind is moving your eyes as you read this book and your hand as you turn the pages. In other words, you're doing PK. More on that thought in a moment.

Psychokinesis is defined as the mind's direct effect on objects and events, on matter and energy, without the use of the physical body or tools. The literal meaning of the word is *mind*, or *mental*, *action* or *movement*. The mind moving or acting upon the physical world.

Traditionally, we think of PK as causing movement of objects, weird energy displays, disruption or enhancement of equipment and technology, levitation, teleportation, metal-bending, and even healing. PK is usually applied as a label to an unusual circumstance when that circumstance happens outside the body.

INTENTION

TO MY MIND, any conscious or unconscious *intention* by the mind that the body actually carries out is psychokinesis. You may wonder how can I say this?

Science and medicine have given us knowledge of neurons firing in the brain and the connections those neurons make with our muscles. When the right neurons fire down the right path, the right parts of our bodies move. But how does our intention, conscious or not, cause the right neurons to fire in the first place? There's something missing in our knowledge of this equation.

For all we know about the human body, we know relatively little about the brain, and less about mind or consciousness. A strictly mechanistic view of the brain and body says we are nothing more than biological machines. Mechanistically, we're programmed for a certain range of actions and sensations, with neurons somehow firing in a pattern that creates the experience of moving our bodies through free will.

But if the brain is merely the place where mind resides, or even the organ that generates the mind, then any intent that sets off physical reactions in the body becomes by definition, mind over matter—or PK.

Science fiction writer Martin Caidin, who was capable of moving items with PK.

PASSING LIMITS

ROGER BANNISTER broke the world's running record for the fastest mile in 1954, passing what was believed the limit of four minutes. Before Bannister, the four-minute mile was thought impossible. But shortly after he showed that humans could push their performance past the supposed limit, others— dozens—also broke the old four-minute record.

The limits we put on physical performance are seemingly one part physical, and one part mental. With some appropriate *intent* and the ability to at least temporarily ignore or shrug off the limitations others place on us, what is impossible becomes possible.

Contrary to the beliefs of many scientists, perhaps we have proven the existence of psychokinesis if we push the definition to include any mind-into-action activities of our own brain-mind and body. By pushing the mind to directly impact the body, we can exceed what society tells us are "normal limits." By pushing further, we can do things with our bodies, as many martial artists do, that seem to break the limits without breaking the body. Setting limitations on what we believe to be our capabilities, whether verbally expressed or merely thought, creates barriers to physical and mental performance. In other words, PK is what we do to surpass the limits we place on ourselves.

WHAT IS PK?

FROM THE PERSPECTIVE of the psychic world, PK covers only those apparent effects of the mind on outside physical things, processes, and forces. To parapsychologists, psychokinetic effects can be broken down into subcategories, which, unlike the abilities categorized under ESP, may be different applications of the same ability rather than separate abilities.

TELEKINESIS

PK COVERS A WIDE RANGE OF EFFECTS, although the one you're probably most familiar with is *telekinesis,* or the ability to move objects from a distance. This can range from simple up-and-down levitation to floating across a room or even flying across the sky— although there have been no reports of anyone doing the latter under her own power lately. Since psychokinetic effects include much more than just levitation, parapsychologists have given up the older term *telekinesis* for the broader one, psychokinesis.

POLTERGEISTS

THE PK PHENOMENON that will receive most of our attention throughout this book is the poltergeist experience. In a poltergeist case, objects are reported to move about under their own power, things break by themselves, sounds are heard, and perhaps some vague forms may

TV producer Jude Gerard Prest was able to move objects after a brief lesson from Martin Caidin.

even be seen lurking about. Originally it was thought that mischievous spirits were responsible, hence the translation of the old German term poltergeist into English as "noisy ghost."

However, parapsychologists now link the teleki-netic effects to a living person or persons, and to a stress-related situation. All the paranormal events have been found to surround a central person, called an *agent*. Most of the events follow a pattern, although the timing of the happenings is generally spontane-ous. Because the events tend to recur, parapsycholo-gist William G. Roll coined the phrase "recurrent spontaneous psychokinesis," or RSPK, to cover this modern model of the poltergeist.

Other larger-scale PK effects include the material-izAtion or dematerialization of objects—including *teleportation*, or what would appear to be the move-ment of an object from one location to another without its having traveled the distance between them. We also have reports of mental impressions—images—having been put onto film or videotape, of film fogged mentally, and of videotape and audiotape erased with a mere thought. Sounds have apparently been produced on audiotape via PK as well.

HEALING

PSYCHIC HEALING IS THE ABILITY to heal oneself or someone else either with amazing speed or with an unexpected outcome, such as the recovery of a terminal cancer patient. This healing may occur through simple concentration or through the laying on of hands. *Psychic surgery* is a phrase applied to the technique of actually opening up the body of a patient with either a sharp instrument or the hands alone. Generally, little or no blood flows, the psychic "surgeon" may manipulate the patient's insides or

perhaps even remove some
malignancy, and the
apparent wound is
healed fairly quickly
or even instantly,
leaving little or no
scar.

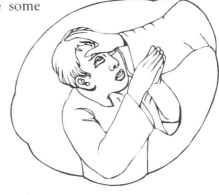

   Parapsychologists
are interested in
psychic healing tech-
niques, especially since the
laying on of hands method has been applied with
success even to blood samples and flasks of enzymes.
However, psychic surgery has not been studied under
laboratory conditions, owing both to ethical considerations—since such practices are not quite kosher in
the United States—and to problems of control related
to the large number of apparently fraudulent practitioners in countries such as Brazil and the Philip-
pines. Since psychic surgery can be easily faked, it is
difficult to study outside the lab.

   With healing, we can see the end result—the
person gets better, the bone knits faster, the wound
heals quickly. However, even though this is observed
by the naked eye, it's likely PK is actually working at
a microscopic level to cause the healing.

SELF HEALING

SELF HEALING is brought easily under the PK banner,
as visualization techniques, psychosomatic illnesses,
and the placebo effect all seem to indicate that our
minds can cause some direct effects in our own
bodies. In psychic healing situations, it's often difficult to determine just who is doing the actual healing: the healer or the patient. Is the healer actually

exerting a paranormal influence on the patient? Or is the healer merely serving as a placebo, stimulating the belief (and often faith) and causing the patient to speed up his own healing process? We don't really know. But we do know that mentally-influenced healing does work.

METAL BENDING

THANKS TO THE POPULARITY of Israeli paranormalist Uri Geller during the 1970s, the apparently psychic bending of metal came into public awareness as a PK effect. In metal-bending a person holds and strokes a spoon or bar of metal, while focusing attention on making it bend. The metal appears to soften and to be easily be manipulated into bent shapes or even tied into knots.

Many people have claimed this ability. In the late 1970s and into the 1980s, spoon-bending parties were all the rage. Attendees would be cheered into a state where they'd yell at their spoons, forks, hacksaw blades, or rods of metal— Bend! Bend! BEND! From there, observers of the attendees saw all sorts of bending going on, though it would often be clear that much of it

The author at a metal-bending "party" .

was happening from strength and pressure, not because of PK.

However, some unusual bending did happen. Metal utensils bent over, sometimes flopped over, by themselves in view of many witnesses. Hacksaw blades, made of a brittle metal that breaks unless the bending happens extremely slowly,

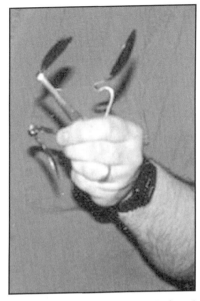

Spoons... bent with telekinetic force?

allowed themselves to be quickly tied into knots. Thick rods or bars of metal were bent easily, even though such bends were beyond the typical limits of human strength.

From a conceptual perspective, any paranormal bending might be a result of some force coming out of the mind affecting the metal's molecular structure. Aerospace engineer Jack Houck worked with a metallurgist to look at the structure of bent metal samples. They found unusual effects on the metal grains when the bends had occurred in what looked like a paranormal way, as compared to metal that was bent simply with sheer strength or leverage. This indicates that the telekinetic force was working on a microscopic level.

HUMAN MACHINE INTERACTIONS

HAVE YOU EVER HAD electronics or even mechanical devices act "weird" around you, especially when you were stressed out or in a hurry? One of the more interesting PK effects became noticed as more and more technology developed and moved into the workplace and the home. From watches to cars to computers, some people have recurring episodes of technology problems.

For years we may have blamed inexplicable equipment malfunctions on Murphy's Law, which states that if anything can go wrong it will. However, there's clear indication that much of what causes many such malfunctions is the operator or owner's moods and stress levels. Research has indicated that technology can be affected—negatively or positively—by the mental state of the operator, or simply by people nearby.

As an example, when I'm under deadline pressure and feeling especially stressed out, or if I'm feeling depressed, I've learned from experience that I need to stay away from my laptop. It behaves oddly, only adding to my frustrations. Of course, this could be a result of my making more mistakes when I'm under such pressure. I hit the wrong keys, some would say. But in reality, I've seen this happen without my touching a single key. I've also observed other devices having problems around myself and others when unusual stress is in the air.

There are studies comparing people who really love computers to those who hate them. The techno-haters have significantly more computer crashes than the techno-loving folks. In one incident I witnessed, computers in a training room crashed whenever an individual who admitted to "really hate those things" got within 3 feet of them. Strangely enough, when I've related the results to people in the computer industry are rarely surprised. In fact, a number have said something like, "Oh yeah, we've known that people's mindset affects computer performance for a long time."

While these effects are often only temporary, they seem to be an indication of a connection between the mind and the technology. Parapsychologists have dubbed these particular PK effects "human–machine interactions." By the way, there are also apparently some folks who can make technology work better. You know the type. They seem to be able to fix things just by putting their hands on the devices.

THE NUMBER OF APPLICATIONS OF THE MIND ON MATTER MAY BE LIMITED ONLY BY OUR IMAGINATION. PK INCLUDES ANY EFFECT ON MATERIAL THINGS OR PROCESSES OR ENERGY CAUSED BY ANY MIND INCLUDING THAT OF A GHOST, OF COURSE, SINCE GHOSTS ARE ALL MIND AND NO BODY.

4
SURVIVAL

ESEARCHERS THEORIZE that part of us—called the personality—survives physical death and use the term Survival for this spiritual phenomenon. For consciousness to survive death it must be different and separable from the brain and the body which die. Some modern philosophers, physicists, parapsychologists, and psychics postulate that consciousness is a result of brain processes that generates a field of energetic interactions, which may be able to continue on after the death of that brain. Some scientists and nonscientists who are more materialistic believe that what we call our mind may actually be a kind of advanced "programming," specialized subroutines programmed into the gray matter of our brain much like a computer is programmed.

Still others suggest that consciousness exists before the body and brain develop. In one view, the brain acts like a TV set that is the receiver of an individual consciousness. Taking this metaphor further, we can say that the brain has limits on how much consciousness it can utilize. Like a TV set that is limited to certain channels—unless one adds a cable or satellite decoder box—so too we experience only part of our potential consciousness because of the brain's limits. Damage to the brain, like damage to a TV set, restricts the flow of consciousness but not the originating signals. The broadcast signals are in the air even if we don't have the right receiver tuned to the right signal.

Can we *prove* that humans have a mind, a consciousness at all—especially one different from animals or even of "thinking" machines like computers? Not at this point. There is no device for detecting a mind. Brain scan devices make images of the physical brain but can not image the mind. Such scans are only indications of activity in the brain.

The fact is that science can't prove the existence of a mind in a body. If science cannot prove the mind exists, it cannot expect to detect consciousness *outside* the body. In other words, we can't prove the existence of ghosts without first proving the existence of consciousness. We can't prove the survival of consciousness after death when we can't prove consciousness exists in the first place. Yet there are phenomena that suggest Survival is possible.

APPARITIONS

A GHOST, OR APPARITION, is consciousness without a body after death of the body. An apparition is what is seen, heard, felt, or smelled and is related to some part of consciousness that can somehow exist in our physical universe after the death of its body. If a presence we experience has true personality or intelligence behind it, we can then consider it a true apparition.

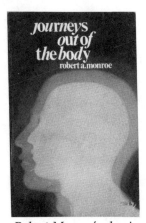

Robert Monroe's classic book about OBEs.

OUT OF BODY

ANOTHER PHENOMENON is the experience of part of the mind or spirit splitting off and leaving the body—the *out-of-the-body experience* (OBE), also called *astral projection*. Out of body experiences occur most frequently during sleep when the person has an experience being awake and physically leaving their body. Sometimes they actually see themselves sleeping in the bed as they float somewhere above. Is.

People who have had OBEs report that it is not actually the soul or spirit that leaves the body, but a part of the mind or consciousness that splits off and travels. Since your spirit never actually vacates the body, the chances of some other entity coming in and taking over while you're "out" are nil—contrary to what some occultists believe.

NEAR DEATH EXPERIENCES

SOME PEOPLE WHO have been clinically dead for a brief time, such as during an operation, feel themselves leaving the body. They report observing the location and people around their seemingly lifeless corpse, before rising up through a sort of tunnel toward an especially bright light. Occasionally, a religious figure or a deceased family member or friend is seen or heard at the end of the tunnel. The person having the experience may be told it is not yet his time, may decide that it is not the right time to die, or may simply know to go back. In any event, the body is resuscitated, and the person finds himself in it, with a recollection of the near-death experience. The near-death experience, or NDE, has attracted much interest even within the medical community.

People are often so impressed by the experience that they change their outlook toward death, toward life, and even toward the people around them. It is a transcendental experience, more than merely the physical reaction or psychological construct. After the near death experience many report psychic experiences or claim to develop various psychic abilities. Not everyone whose heart stops has an NDE, however

REINCARNATION

ANOTHER FORM OF SURVIVAL IS the rebirth of the soul in another body, or reincarnation. The ancient idea of the spirit or soul being reborn in another body is accepted in some form by many world's religions. In fact, it's been stated that well over a billion people believe in some kind of reincarnation.

Most suggestive of reincarnation are those cases involving very young children who "remember" their past lives spontaneously, without any prompting. Children between two and four years old have developed neither a strong individual personality nor a great stock of memories. So when they suddenly speak of a past life, often with substantial details, one must sit up and take notice. Unfortunately, such children don't keep the memories of their past lives very long, as their own personality starts to exert itself and submerges this information.

Psychiatrist, Brian Weiss, is a leading proponent of reincarnation.

Many believe that they can contact the dead through the Ouija Board.

COMMUNICATION WITH THE DEAD

MEDIUMSHIP, the phenomenon in which a living person acts as an intermediary between the worlds of the living and the dead, has drawn a great deal of attention from the early psychical research. The medium is at the center of the communications or is the actual channel through which contact is made. Mediumistic phenomena are divided into three areas, according to the three kinds of mediums, *physical*, *mental*, and *psychic*.

PHYSICAL MEDIUMS

PHYSICAL MEDIUMS BRING ABOUT physical disturbances along with verbal messages from the dead. Physical medium sessions are characterized by tables tilting or rising, objects floating, apparitional sightings, table and wall raps, objects appearing or disappearing, floating lights, and even ectoplasm—almost always a non-slimy variety.

Physical mediums have declined in popularity, possible as a result of the investigations and exposures of so many phony mediums during the early part of the 20th Century. The seance

A common feature of seances was asking the sitters to place their hands on the table, which would raise in the air.

scam was a good way to get money out of grieving relatives, who tend to be extremely credulous. When investigators showed interest in the phenomena, some mediums attempted ambitious fraud in the hope of a good "grade" as a medium—an excellent reference for future business. Unfortunately for the mediums, too many of these investigators had more than a little knowledge of fraudulent psychic techniques. A few of them were full-time professional magicians or brought such fraud-busters with them.

The rise of motion pictures and other technological marvels—especially those used for entertainment contributed to the decline of physical mediumship. People have simply found other ways to amuse and scare themselves than to sit in the dark waiting for the spirits to do something.

MENTAL MEDIUMS

MENTAL MEDIUMS claim to speak directly with the dead. They often go into an altered state, allowing spirits to use their bodies and speak through them. Sittings with mental mediums are generally not quite as flashy as those with the physical mediums, but the information coming through to the sitters—those visiting the medium and trying to contact the dead—can be more detailed and certainly more relevant than mere floating tables.

Psychic Annette Martin communicates with ghost of Café Van Kleef, Oakland, CA.

Stereotypically mental mediums go into trance to get in touch with their particular "control" entity, who acts like an other-worldly telephone operator to contact the lost loved one. Information from the departed soul may come through in a variety of ways. It may be spoken directly through the mouth of the medium—a sort of person-to-person call—or the medium may repeat what she is told to say by the control, which has been given the words of the spirit contacted. Sometimes the trance medium has the words passed directly from the contacted spirit, without the use of a control spirit.

PSYCHIC MEDIUMS

RECENTLY, MEDIUMS HAVE STEERED AWAY from entering trance to being fully conscious. These mediums claim that their psychic abilities allow them to perceive a deceased person who comes to the sitter. No control entity and no trance are necessary, as these mediums are simply receiving information from the deceased and passing it along. The information can be quite spotty, as the psychic processes of these mediums can distort the information or not be wide open to it.

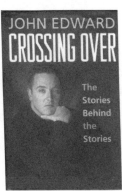

John Edwards amazed TV viewers with his messages from departed relatives.

In the late 1990s, the popularity of psychic mediums grew to a point where, in the early part of the 21st Century, a number of these folks regularly appeared on television. James Van Praagh and John Edward had popular TV series. Other mediums—Rosemary Altea, George Anderson, and Sylvia Browne—appeared on talk and news programs, becoming celebrities.

AUTOMATIC WRITING

IN AUTOMATIC WRITING, the medium's hand writes on its own without conscious control. In fact, a great deal of information has been written automatically, such is the *Seth Material* volumes by the late Jane Roberts. Even Victor Hugo, author of *The Hunchback of Notre Dame*, is reputed to have relied extensively on automatic writing. Some mediums produce drawings and paintings automatically. Brazilian Luis Gasparetto paints automatically, claiming the spirits of dead artists work through him.

CHANNELING

FOR A TIME, channeling was at the forefront of the psychic world. A broader term than mediumship, *channeling* may refer to speaking with the departed, but more often it refers to those who psychically or spiritually contact other-than-human entities. Such channeled entities are claimed to be representative of alien intelligences, group spirit minds, dolphins, other-dimensional beings, or the extremely long dead, like warlords from Atlantis.

Channeling, while an interesting phenomenon in its own right, is generally not suggestive of Survival, however. Many channeled entities claim to be alive at the time of the channeling. Others are too long dead or from too far away—other galaxies or dimensions that attempt to verify information about them, or where they came from is futile.

Interest in Survival of bodily death is on the rise. Researchers are encouraged to conduct scientific study of the evidence for our continued existence beyond death. Interest in Survival played such an important role in the evolution of parapsychology, and in our understanding of apparitions, hauntings, and poltergeists.

5

BEGINNINGS

ACKGROUND INFORMATION about parapsychology as a field of investigation is helpful to understand why parapsychologists do what they do. This chapter lays some groundwork, although it cannot do justice to more than a century of research and investigation.

Throughout history the use of psychic abilities has made its mark on life-styles across a wide range of human culture and religion. Our fascination with death and life after death, coupled with a longing to believe that death is not the end of our existence, has sustained our permanent fascination for ghosts and all things spiritual.

BIRTH OF PARAPSYCHOLOGY

THE SOCIETY FOR PSYCHICAL RESEARCH (SPR) was founded in London in 1882. It didn't appear out of a vacuum; two major trends began in the mid-1800s that kick-started the SPR. These were the burgeoning spiritualist movement and the rise of rational empiricism in science.

Rational and empirical thought in science at the time shaped how early researchers looked at the phenomena. Their aim was to collect empirical data about the psychic and spiritual events in the world so that they could explain another part of the vast range of human experience. However, it was the spiritualist movement that really set the stage for just what would be studied.

THE SPIRITUALIST MOVEMENT

WHILE SPIRITUAL PHENOMENA had been evident for thousands of years, it was the experiences of the Fox sisters near Rochester, New York, that ignited the spiritualist movement. The two young girls demonstrated some kind of contact with spirits when questions they asked were answered with rapping noises.

PHOTO FROM *WANDERINGS OF A SPIRITUALIST* BY SIR ARTHUR CONAN-DOYLE, RONIN PUBLISHING.

Sir Arthur Conan-Doyle, author of Sherlock Holms, was a Spiritualist— shown here in 1920 .

People were amazed and delighted at this evidence of spirit contact. The wave of interest spread slowly in the United States, but jumped the ocean to Great Britain, where the SPR was founded. Here in the States, while the movement was less organized, there were upsurges of interest in spirit contact during and after the War Between the States and the First

World War. With so many lives lost during warfare, there was a natural urge for people who had lost loved ones to try to contact them. Among the founders and early members of the SPR were both well-respected scientists and intellectual spiritualists.

The original leadership established several committees to investigate thought transference (telepathy) and clairvoyance, gifted subjects (both psychics and mediums), hypnotism and its apparent effects, apparitions and hauntings, physical phenomena (from poltergeists to physical mediumship), and studies of literature, investigating the literary and historical roots of ideas on the phenomena.

In 1885, the American Society for Psychical Research (ASPR) was founded in Boston, and later moved to New York. Famed psychologist William James and astronomer-mathematician Simon Newcomb inspired the formation of the ASPR, with Newcomb as its first president.

PSYCHICAL RESEARCH AND MEDIUMS

BETWEEN THE 1880s AND 1920, the major thrust of psychical research was an interest in the phenomena brought to

The God-Speed luncheon in London in 1920, where 250 out of 290 guests stood as testimoney that they were in personal touch with their dead.

PHOTO FROM *WANDERINGS OF A SPIRITUALIST* BY SIR ARTHUR CONAN-DOYLE, RONIN PUBLISHING.

light by spiritualist mediums. Many of the early investigators were quite stubborn and skeptical, brought up important questions: Was the information received by a medium passed by an actual spirit entity, or does it come through the medium's own clairvoyant reception of that information from psychic "records" or does it come from living sources. The early investigators looked at telepathy as *the* way for a spirit to communicate, since as it was obvious that a spirit lacks the physical means to talk.

In the 1920s, Psychologist William McDougall became president of the ASPR, and one of the two people largely responsible for the rise of what we call parapsychology. McDougall's influence on the other important figure, a young biologist by the name of Joseph Banks Rhine, led Rhine to follow him to Duke University.

An internal conflict in the ASPR over a medium called "Margery" brought the controversy over fraudulent mediums to a head. The fascination of some of the ASPR's more prominent members with the antics of

Early 20th Century medium commanding a table to rise,
supposedly with the help of spirits.

medium Mina Crandon of Boston caused a wide split in the attitudes of members and outside observers alike.

Margery could seemingly produce a wide range of effects in a darkened seance room, including levitations, glowing ectoplasm, ringing bells and the linking of wooden rings. An investigation by a committe sent by *Scientific American,* was anything but unanimous. Harry Houdini and William McDougall and other dissenters claimed Margery was faking it all. Houdini took to duplicating her feats, including those produced while she was sealed in a wooden box with only her head sticking through an opening. Was Margery real or a fraud? The controversy has raged on causing a split in the group that lasted for years.

By keeping a skeptical, noncommittal attitude about her genuineness as a medium McDougall and Rhine were able to avoid becoming embroiled in the scandalous situation of the Margery mediumship. Rhine himself later became the acknowledged "father" of parapsychological research.

THE RHINES AT DUKE

J.B. AND LOUISA RHINE came to Duke University with McDougal in 1927. They wanted to move research from the seance parlor to the laboratory, Rhine began experiments in what he called extra-sensory perception and psychokinesis. The three were quite focused on making studies of psychic phenomena acceptable to the academic world. The parapsychology laboratory was started at Duke in 1935

Their research focused on proving the existence of psi. To utilize statistics and eliminate sensory cues, Rhine developed research techniques using Karl Zener's ESP cards, which are a set of five cards with

Karl Zener's ESP cards, which are no longer used in parapsychological testing.

five basic symbols, one on each card. This one-in-five choice made statistical analysis easy, and provided subjects with simple choices. The researchers noticed specific effects in the data. "Psi-missing" is a score significantly below chance. "Decline effect" refers to the decline of a subject's scores toward chance over a number of trials. These observations led the researchers to investigate attitude and personality influences on the occurrence of psi.

Rhine's team wished to do more than merely *see* psi at work. They sought patterns and explanations for the displays of apparent psychic phenomena in the world outside the lab that the investigators witnessed. They gathered data that they hoped would

Joseph Banks Rhine and Louisa Rhine, who might be called the parents of parapsychology, in their office at Duke University.

lead to answers to prove the existence of these newly investigated phenomena of ESP and PK. They also hoped to show the universal nature of psychic abilities, that all people shared the talents evidenced by so-called psychics and mediums.

Rhine trained a whole generation of psi researchers. His laboratory produced an enormous amount of statistical evidence and established new levels of controls for research in parapsychology.

Rhine retired in 1965 and severed his formal ties with Duke, and set up the Foundation for Research on the Nature of Man, with its Institute for Parapsychology. Some years after Rhine's death in 1980 the Foundation was renamed the Rhine Research Foundation, in honor of both the Rhines.

OTHER RESEARCHERS

THE RHINES WERE NOT THE FIRST RESEARCHERS to give psychic phenomena the laboratory treatment. In France, Rene Warcollier conducted telepathy experiments with senders who focused on drawings. In the United States, psychologist John Coover conducted various ESP experiments in a laboratory at Stanford University, under funding by Thomas Stanford. One of his more interesting studies focused on the phenomenon of a person's knowing when she is being stared at—a commonly reported experience, and one that is the subject of much current parapsychological research.

During the Rhine era, attitudes of the public shifted. People still went to mediums, psychics, and fortune-tellers, but in a more private manner. Technology seemed to make those practices appear ridiculous, especially in light of the fraud controversies surrounding so many mediums.

In the 1940s, Dr. Gertrude Schmeidler, one of the pioneers of research into the process behind psi, looked at how it works and who is more psychic. She formulated the "sheep-goat effect," which postulates that belief indicates for the way one will score in a psi test. Believers, or "sheep," have a tendency to score above chance, and nonbelievers, or "goats," tend to score below chance, often significantly.

The Parapsychology Foundation was founded in 1951 and incorporated by Eileen Garrett, herself a medium and author. Her mission was to further the study of psychic phenomena and the dissemination of information about those studies. Eileen Garrett died in 1970, but the Foundation is still run by her "spirit" in the form of her family.

The Parapsychological Association was founded in 1957 and is currently the world's only organization of professional parapsychologists and people with a professional interest in scientific research of psi. Although there are a few exceptional researchers and

PHOTO FROM WANDERINGS OF A SPIRITUALIST BY SIR ARTHUR CONAN-DOYLE, RONIN PUBLISHING.

Laying corner stone of Spiritualist church in Brisbane, Australia in 1921.

investigators who are not members of that organization, the overwhelming majority of reputable researchers are members, or are well-known to members. In 1969 the organization was admitted to the American Association for the Advancement of Science.

RECENT DEVELOPMENTS

INTEREST IN FIELD INVESTIGATIONS EXPANDED in the latter 20th Century as methods of investigation grew up. Much of the way parapsychologists look at psi as it occurs outside the laboratory has changed because of what was learned in the years of experimental research. Today, many laboratory researchers also have an interest in spontaneous cases of psi. Naturally, those like myself who specialize in spontaneous cases are still interested in laboratory experimentation and continue to monitor what's going on in that area.

Research in parapsychology has shifted into and out of labs, with research centers coming and going, mostly owing to the scarcity of funding. While a few labs are still going strong in the United States—notably the Rhine Research Center in North Carolina, the Princeton Engineering Anomalies Research (PEAR) lab in New Jersey, and the Institute of Noetic Sciences in northern California—it's Great Britain that's seeing the greatest resurgence of parapsychological research in the early 21st Century.

In the arena of survival of bodily death, interest has remained high, especially on the part of the general public. Most parapsychologists have stayed in the laboratory, but a few have done more than their share in researching issues related to Survival. For example, research into reincarnation has gone on for decades at the University of Virginia. In addition, research with mediums, trance and psychic type, is back in vogue both in the United States and the United Kingdom. However, instead of doing the research in the seance room, researchers are working with their medium-subjects in controlled settings.

There is a wide range and diversity in the kinds of research done by parapsychologists and the orientations of the various parapsychological groups around the world. Although funding sources have unfortunately been few and far between, the advent of the Internet has allowed for a new spreading and discussion of ideas, experiments, and experiences. Groups of researchers and practitioners "meet" on the Internet to discuss issues of Survival, research considerations, and applications of psi.

Connections to Other Sciences

IN SPITE OF THE TERM "PARAPSYCHOLOGY," many other sciences besides psychology add to our understanding of psi, and psi has many implications for them. Influences on how parapsychologists look at psi can be seen in the diverse backgrounds of parapsychologists. While a majority of the members of the Parapsychological Association have academic backgrounds in psychology, many other areas are repre-sented as well. These include physics, anthropology, biology, sociology, philosophy, physiology, chemistry, pharmacology, education, and psychiatry. Parapsy-chology, contrary to a misconception common to the media and the Internet, is not "paranormal psychology."

Spirits and science kicked off the field, which has now become somewhat interdisciplinary. That parapsychology cuts across so many fields is appropriate, given that psi itself demonstrates the inter-connectedness of us all.

6

IN THE LAB

ETAILING THE RANGE OF PAST and present experiments in parapsychology is beyond the scope of this book. Instead, I will touch on a few key research trends and some findings that relate to our ghostly phenomena.

PROOF RESEARCH

IMAGES OF CARD GUESSING AND DICE ROLLING generally come to mind when people think of ESP and PK research. Actually, researchers abandoned such testing procedures decades ago. Mainstream science did not—and still does not—accept psi's existence, though many believe the evidence is certainly there in favor of psi. Much of the original research by Rhine and his colleagues was directed at proving that psi existed. This kind of research was known as *proof* research. Several interesting perceptions came out of Rhine's research, and the proof research that followed.

THE DECLINE EFFECT

RHINE IDENTIFIED WHAT IS KNOWN AS the *decline effect* wherein scores may start out above chance for subjects, but then decline, eventually reaching chance. One explanation is that it is the result of a human response to doing a repetitive task. People taking psi tests over and over again seem to get bored. Certainly you would after making hundreds of guesses about what symbol is on a card. In fact, the boredom effect is observable in many psychology experiments and in the testing of human performance.

Another obstacle to research has been zeroing in on only one phenomenon. When research-ers attempted to test for telepathy they quickly realized that one could not separate te-lepathy from clairvoyance. The receiver might be picking up the information from the actual target (clairvoyance) rather than the mind of the sender (telepathy). Whether or not one uses a sender—someone looking at or thinking of the target—seems to be irrelevant in many cases.

Psi Missing

SCORING WELL BELOW THE ODDS IS SIGNIFICANT and not just chance. Just as with scores above the odds, scores below the odds suggest that something besides chance is operating. Rhine coined the term *psi-missing* for those scoring significantly below chance. If the odds were one in five, which is 20%, then we would expect about 20 out of every 100 guesses to be correct. People getting a few correct answers below or above 20 are still consid-ered to be scoring at chance level. But imagine scor-ing only one correct answer out of 100 guesses.

Statistically, that is quite significant, which means not by chance. Something is influencing them... something believed to be psi.

POWER OF BELIEF

GERTRUDE SCHMEIDLER IDENTIFIED the *sheep-goat effect.* Believers in psi—sheep—tend to score above chance; disbelievers—goats—tend to score at chance or often below. Interestingly, it turns out that many who were psi-missing were disbelievers. It's as though their subconscious minds knew the answers via psi but did not want to give the researchers any data that might prove psi's existence The sheep-goat effect is quite consistent across ESP and PK experiments. It even shows up in experiments and displays of human performance. People who believe a task is possible perform better than those who don't. People who believe they can personally do a task consistently performed at a higher level than do those who believe someone else can do it, but not themselves.

J.B. Rhine focused on laboratory studies, while Louisa Rhine was more interested in psi as it occurred in the world outside the lab.

Modern parapsychologists are well aware of the role belief plays, not only in research but also in cases of apparitions, hauntings, and poltergeists. Believers tend to be much better receivers of signals from apparent apparitions and of imprints in haunting cases. In poltergeist cases, what one believes can support or shut down the PK activity of the subconscious.

In the latter part of the 20th Century, research moved away from *proof* to *process*. Parapsychologists became more interested in understanding how psi works in different situations, for different tasks, and for different people. What makes one person more psychic than others became a central research question.

Research tasks shifted from simple card guessing to other kinds of less rigid imagery. Instead of providing limited, or forced, choices, tests became more like things one encounters in real life, especially in studying receptive psi. Pictures and objects, and eventually locations were chosen as targets, for example. Controlled studies of remote viewing have been fruitful. Researchers have demonstrated that images with more emotional content—things that get us aroused, good or bad—make better targets. Another intriguing finding is that after subjects get past the initial "I can't do that" response almost all subjects can pick up some perceptual details about target locations.

Parapsychology is not about psychics with Tarot cards.

MACRO AND MICRO

PSYCHOKMETIC EXPERIMENTS ARE DIVIDED into two subgroups of PK, known as *macro-* and *micro-PK* effects. Macro-PK effects are those that can be seen, such as levitation, metal-bending, or dematerialization of objects. Poltergeist phenomena usually fit here. Micro-PK effects occur on a microscopic or even subatomic level, requiring sophisticated equipment to keep track of them—more sensitive than the naked eye.

Sometimes it is difficult to determine if a PK effect is happening on a large or small scale. A photo seemingly affected by PK of a subject—or a ghost—may be an effect of the mind on the chemical grains on the film. So while we see the end result—the photo—the PK is occurring at the microscopic level. Psychic healing is another example. We may observe a macro-level result, while the cause occurs at the cellular level—microscopic.

STUDYING SMALL

THE DISTINCTION BETWEEN THE MACROSCOPIC and micro-scopic levels is fairly inefficient, except when the labels are applied to the kinds of PK research parapsychologists conduct.

Generally micro-PK studies are conducted with a random-number or random-event generator hooked into some kind of device that offers feedback to the subject. A computer or some other instrument to monitor the effect is hooked into a device that generates a random signal. Such a device might include a radioactive element that, over a specified period of time, might give off a particle or might not—something like the toss of a coin. The subject tries to affect the system so as to make the effect no longer random—resulting in more heads than tails, for example.

Micro-PK studies are popular among parapsychologists because the experimental conditions are simpler and can be easily controlled. Macro-PK studies are more like what happens outside the lab, which makes them particularly interesting. But they're more difficult to control, since there are many ways to simulate or fake the same effect. The spontaneous PK effects on computers and other devices are much like what is being studied with technology in the lab.

RESEARCH TODAY

MODERN PARAPSYCHOLOGICAL RESEARCH INCLUDES a variety of methodologies. Remote viewing research continues. Presentiment research which investigates the possibility that considering whether we are unconsciously aware of upcoming events—at the level of our bodies—is a popular trend. Healing research is on the upswing.

The author with associate Dr. Kathy Dalton, setting up an experiment with psychic Aiko Gibo.

Being Stared At

Most of us can tell when we are stared at. But what if we were in another room? If someone were watching us via a TV hidden camera, would we detect it? Current research is looking at this in a unique way, considering both conscious and unconscious awareness.

Subjects who are targets of the staring are hooked up to physiological measures. They sit in a room and register times when they think they are being watched via video system that gives no clues as to whether or not someone is watching them. The person doing the staring looks at a monitor that is controlled by a computer system. Sometimes the screen is blank; sometimes the target subject is shown from the back. When the person staring sees the subject, he focuses all his attention on the subject—staring hard.

The computer tracks these monitor on-off periods and compares them to the physiological data from the subject. The results so far show that people's bodies react to being stared at, which suggests an awareness of being stared at on the unconscious level. In apparition cases, this may be what causes us to sense a presence. The ghost perceives us, and we are aware of that.

Global Consciousness

An interesting project that is essentially open to the public is the Global Consciousness Project (GCP), which studies how emotion-causing world events affect random event generators placed around the world. This project is researching the idea of global mind change and if there is some kind of global mind—a consensus of all our consciousness—that can affect the world around us.

The GCP involves researchers from several labs and institutions from a number of different countries. It's an international effort considering whether we are somehow interconnected on the level of consciousness and whether that can be scientifically investigated and even proven. We might consider this a global poltergeist effect, though the PK is only working on specific targets, the random event generators.

After Life Experiments

Dr. Gary Schwartz and colleagues at the Human Energy Systems Laboratory at the University of Arizona conducted lab research with several spirit mediums in the late 1990s. He asked mediums to communicate with any spirits that appeared around the target subjects. Target subjects rated how well the mediums did in coming up with information about the spirit— usually a relative—and the subject during this encounter.

Schwartz explored possible feedback the subjects unconsciously provided and developed a method for scoring the readings. The research has slowly progressed to a point where more elaborate controls are being used to avoid feedback to the medium and the possibility that the mediums, consciously or unconsciously, make general statements that can fit many potential subjects.

The test subjects are psychic mediums. Instead of going into trance, they claim to psychically perceive the spirits around the target subjects. This is much the same as a psychic working with a ghost hunter on an apparition investigation. Schwartz's research has some real connection to field investigations of apparitions.

The next step for Schwartz and his lab might be to set up a situation where the spirit being communicated with can be subject to some of the same technology ghost hunters use in investigations.

APPARITIONS

PPARITIONS ARE CONSCIOUS, THINKING beings existing after the death of their bodies and capable of some form of communication with the living. People who have seen ghosts have not reported them to be like white-sheeted, cloudy figures, nor are they green, hot-dog-gobbling figures. True apparitions are often more startling than what is in old ghost stories.

Ghosts look like people, like you and me. Sometimes they may be a bit fuzzy around the edges—sort of an out-of-focus image, or a bit on the see-through side. Those are exceptions. In general, reported apparitions are in 3-D and look like solid citizens. Apparitions usually run from the tops of the head to just around the knees, with the feet missing.

In some encounters, you may not realize that you are looking at an apparition, unless the figure suddenly vanishes before your eyes or you happen to notice the feet missing. Apparitions have a habit of appearing and disappearing from view. You may turn around and someone is suddenly there. A quick look away—the figure vanishes. You might never see the appearing or disappearing process, but the figure looks real enough.

PERCEIVING APPARITIONS

SEEING AN APPARITION IS MORE COMMON than most other encounters, with perhaps the exception of *sensing* the presence of another entity. The reason may be that people rely so heavily on the sense of sight. People also report hearing voices of apparitions, sometimes with a visual presence, sometimes not. Olfactory apparitions—the smell of a perfume, cologne, or some other scent clearly associated with the person the ghost represents—are another form.

Feeling or sensing something is common. You might sense a presence around or you get the feeling you are being stared at with no apparent cause. People report feeling cold chills in the presence of ghosts, though rarely can a physical cold spot be

The Moss Beach Distillery, south of San Francisco, is a restaurant haunted by the apparition of a murdered young woman.

measured. The cold chill, like all other sensations of the ghost, is perceptual rather than physical.

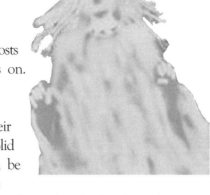

In most cultures, ghosts appear with their clothes on. After all, most humans think of themselves this way. Apparitions and their clothing appear to be solid and reportedly may even be touched or smelled. The apparitional form may be identical with the form the person had in physical existence, or may look younger and possibly healthier.

The size and stature of apparitions appear normal—they never seem to shrink or grow, although their age and physical appearance may relate to another period of their life, and may even change from time to time. In one of my cases, the apparition had been seen as a girl of about 6, as a teenager, and as the old woman she was at the time of her death.

Several people may see the apparition at the same time, with differing perspectives. One witness may see the figure's front, while another, standing behind the appari-tion, sees it from the rear—as though a living person was actually standing there.

Apparitions may react to people and surroundings in the same way a living person would. And why not? If we are really talking about a mind without a body, presumably that mind once *had* a body and interacted with people in the world. If the personality is intact enough to appear as human, then the reactions will be within a fairly normal range, with a few variations of course, such as appearing and disappearing at will.

The author with psychic Annette Martin, attempting to detect the ghost of the Blue Lady at the Moss Beach Distillery.

In some cases different witnesses experience the apparition differently. One person may see the apparition and even hear her voice. Someone else may only hear the voice. Others may smell perfume seemingly coming from where the ghost is seen. Still others may simply feel a presence, actually feel the ghost has touched them, or have that often-reported cold chill. In other words, everyone seems to process the information coming from the apparition in different ways, with different combinations of sight, hearing, smell, and touch but thankfully, not taste.

Four Classes of Apparitions

THERE ARE FOUR MAIN KINDS OF APPARITIONAL experiences: apparitions of the dead, crisis apparitions, deathbed apparitions, and apparitions of the living. These categories are fairly broad, and go back to the work of G. N. M. Tyrrell.

Dead Folks

FIRST AND FOREMOST ARE APPARITIONS OF THE DEAD. These are people who have finished the process of dying and have usually been dead for awhile and are referred to as *postmortem* apparitions. These are the most controversial and the rarest kind of apparition.

The controversy has to do with basic arguments surrounding the existence of consciousness itself, and the possibility that it can exist without a body. Another debate is the question of apparitions represent the consciousness of a deceased person or some kind of hallucination created through a process of ESP and PK?

The Moss Beach Distillery as it existed in the late 1920s, site of a murder that led to a decades long visitation by an apparition.

APPARITIONAL HAUNTINGS

HAUNTINGS ARE SOMETIMES CLASSED as a subset of postmortems apparitions, where the reoccurring figure of the deceased is actually a kind of image imprinted into a geographical location, a house, or an object. Tyrrell assigned these apparitions to a class of their own, as ghosts that haunt a particular location, but a more modern approach differentiates between these and true conscious apparitions.

IN A CRISIS

A SECOND CLASS IS THE *CRISIS APPARITION*, which appears to others when the person represented by the apparition is undergoing a crisis or dangerous situation. The most prevalent crisis is the process of dying, but crisis apparitions have been reported when the individual is trapped because of an accident, severely injured, or very ill. Many times the person represented by the apparition does not die, which means that they are apparitions of the living in such instances.

DEATHBED APPARITIONS

THE MOST COMMON type of apparitions are those of the dying or very recently dead. The time frame is typically from the moments the person is dying to 48 hours after their death. There are many reports of friends or acquaintances who have seen or dreamed the appearance of someone they knew, only to have the person vanish, leaving behind the sense that something harmful had happened. A phone call or letter or e-mail confirms that the apparition appeared at the same time or shortly after the person died or became severely injured.

In general, these apparitions appear to people who know the person. Most often, there's some emotional tie, as with a relative, loved one or a close friend.

Living Ghosts?

THE LAST CATEGORY RELATES TO APPARITIONS OF someone definitely alive, and generally not in crisis. There are two subgroups. In *spontaneous* apparitions of the living, the person does not intend to appear as a projection. Such an appearance is often associated with an out-of-body experience. The individual having an OBE "travels" to another location and is perceived by others. Such apparitional projections can happen when the individual is dreaming.

The other subgroup is the *experimental*—or deliberate—variety, in which the person intends to be seen or perceived in this fashion. The designation *experimental* does not necessarily mean that the apparition appears in the context of a formal experiment.

Observers may encounter the apparition of someone they know who is actively trying to contact them. For example, the apparition may be that of a little girl trying to tell her mother that she is sick. Or the apparition may represent someone having an OBE who is *deliberately* trying to contact other people.

HOUSE GHOSTS

WHILE MOST PEOPLE TEND TO ASSOCIATE GHOSTS with specific locations, such as houses, restaurants, and hotels, apparitions may not tie themselves down to one location. In some cases, the apparition seems to be attached to an individual or even an entire family, following them from place to place. This is not necessarily a bad thing, since the apparition may be there because of personal, emotional attachments. In some cultures and religions, a spirit of an ancestor is expected to follow you around as a sort of spiritual guardian.

Apparitions haunting a location can still be mobile. They may spend most of their time at one place, yet still be reported moving about the neighborhood, or to other locations farther away. In general, apparitions stay with locations they had some association with when alive—though they may have more than one favorite haunt to visit.

THEY DO KNOW THEY ARE DEAD?

ONE COMMON MISCONCEPTION is that they do not know that they are dead and that it is up to the living to help them become aware of this, and then to help them move on to whatever awaits them in the afterlife. Cases reported and investigated by many parapsychologists and psychics contradict this notion. While I've met investigators who had never had such cases—luck of the draw, I'm guessing—I and many others have had cases in which the apparitions clearly communicated the self-awareness of their actual nonliving state. They knew they were dead.

The reasons they give for sticking around as ghosts run the gamut from a fear of what's next, to a sense that staying where they are is somehow "better," to simply feeling more comfortable and safe by sticking with a location or family. Often it is an emotional bond to a person or place that is reported. Apparitions seem to sometimes be present when unusual physical PK activity takes place. In some instances, the apparition is a bystander. In others, it appears the apparition has developed PK.

THE BLUE LADY

A GOOD EXAMPLE IS THE CASE OF THE BLUE LADY, a famous ghost at the Moss Beach Distillery Restaurant south of San Francisco. This woman, murdered in the early 1930s in a lovers' triangle, has communicated to many people that she stayed in and about the restaurant because she loved the place so much when she was alive. It was the site of her long affair with a piano player after leaving her husband, so she has romantic associations with the place. She also communicated that she is waiting for that lost love

The beach below the Distillery, location of the actual murder.

to find her, even though she is aware that after all this time that it is not likely to happen.

Do we make her move on to another existence or another location? If she were responsible for living people being uncomfortable, afraid, or otherwise negatively affected, I would try to reconcile the negative experience of the living. After that, I'd work to move her on.

I feel strongly that if there are no negative effects for the living, and the apparition doesn't want to move along even after being presented with that option, investigators, researchers, and psychics shouldn't force the ghost out. Ghosts have rights, too—or should.

COMMUNICATION

APPARITIONS ARE INTERACTIVE AND COMMUNICATE with us living folks. The communication may be verbal, as someone hears what the apparition is saying. Sometimes it is visual, with the ghost communicating through gestures. With some people, the communication seems to be empathic, in which the witnesses feels what the apparition as feeling or is trying to get across. On occasion, the communication is non-

verbal and nonemotional, with ideas, concepts, and images appearing in the minds of the witnesses.

If you encounter a ghost, try to remain calm. Try to communicate with her, especially if she's trying to communicate with you. The communication process, like the process by which the apparition is perceived in the first place, is related to psi. As ghosts are people too, in everything but physical form, it's important to treat the apparition as a person. Just as you might be afraid of the apparition, you may be scaring it as well.

But don't be afraid. Keep in mind that you have much more to fear from living intruders than ghostly ones, especially since you may have your own built-in psychic defense mechanisms. Ghosts don't carry guns or knives. No one has been seriously hurt by a ghost. There is rarely any harm done to an observer at all, unless the harm is caused by poor judgment due to being afraid—and their ensuing clumsiness.

8

Apparitions and Psi

HERE ARE TWO SIDES to every ghostly sighting. The witness perceives the apparition and apparently the apparition perceives the living witness. Apparitions are capable of verbal communication as well as other forms of interactions.

Differing Perceptions

NOT EVERYONE SEES THE GHOST. Some people only hear a voice; others smell the perfume. Some witnesses have reported being able to "touch" the ghost. What this suggests is that the apparition's "body" can not actually be reflecting light, or putting out sound waves, or emitting physical smells, otherwise witnesses would perceive the same thing—or at least something similar.

Perhaps the occultists are right and there exists an "astral body" composed of some invisible energy or matter. If this is the case an apparition is seen because the witness is psychic enough to "see" it, whereas others—including the camera—do not. Perhaps this is, as some psychics say, because the nonobservers are not tuned in, or they do not believe enough to receive the information. The phenomenon is akin to that of a haunting, where some people seem to be sensitive enough to the recorded information to receive the replay of past events, while others are not.

Cameras and Audio Recorders

Some occultists point out that cameras do pick up ghostly images when the "conditions are right" or when the "ghost wants to show herself to the camera," but they have no model to explain how this is so. A number of ghost hunters report that some audio recorders can pick up the voices of ghosts under certain conditions, or in certain frequency ranges beyond the hearing of humans.

Annette Martin communicating with the Blue Lady of the Distillery out on the patio. Note spots of light on her & the author in this Polaroid shot.

Cameras pick up reflected light, with some do picking up light beyond the spectrum visible to us. Audio recorders have a specific range of sound they pick up, though again some are designed to record sound above or below the normal range of humans. But in each case, we're talking about picking up something physical—a light or sound wave that actually exists.

USING PSI

LET US LOOK AT WHAT WE ASSUME a ghost to be: a part—or all—of the human mind that can exist in the physical world outside the physical body. This energy field floats around apart from the body, unable to interact with people or things in the usual way—no hands, eyes, ears, mouth, or other physical means. This suggests many questions. How can such an entity receive information, let alone be seen as an apparition? How does an energy form reflect light yet still not be seen by the naked eye or the cameras operating at the same time? How does an apparition, who has no larynx or other physical structure to move air to create sound, speak into an audio recorder? By using psi, naturally.

Psi represents interactions of the mind with other minds or the environment that take place apart from such normal physical organs as hands, eyes, ears, or mouth. ESP and PK occur in the living. The mind seems to be able to pull in information from unknown channels and can interact with and reach out to the environment and thus influence it. Considering an apparition as a disembodied mind, without the constraints placed on psi by the brain, it makes sense that psi provides the information and interaction modalities for it to communicate and create physical impact.

TELEPATHY

CURIOUSLY, GHOSTS ARE RARELY IF EVER SEEN in the nude. They appear fully clothed, and may even change clothing on subsequent appearances. They may change their form, to appear as they looked at different stages of their lives. Unless someone out there knows of an ectoplasmic department store on the spiritual plane, we have to wonder, "Where do the clothes and accessories come from?"

The answer comes if we label the communication between apparitions and living folks as telepathic. It's the mind of the ghost communicating to the minds of the witnesses. Apparently apparitions have no particular form other than what they themselves conjure up as their own self-image. In other words, how the entity thinks of or visualizes herself is how the rest of us visually perceive the ghost.

Try this: close your eyes and get a picture of yourself in your mind's eye. That's probably how the living would see you if you were a ghost. Did you visualize yourself with clothing? That's why ghosts don't appear in the nude: self-images in our culture include clothing, with rare exceptions. Did you visualize your whole body? What about your feet and shoes? My experience in asking lecture audiences this question is that most people don't picture their feet when visualizing themselves. It is interesting that most apparitions are not seen below the knees.

Apparitions communicate on a telepathic basis, essentially broadcasting their self-images and messages. Our receptive psi processes pick up this self-image, which is added to information received by our normal senses. Information from the psi process and the senses gets mixed in the process of perception.

Some of us can process this telepathic input better on a visual basis, others auditorially, others through feeling or even on an olfactory basis. Many can experience a ghost on multiple sensory levels— seeing and hearing the apparition at the same time.

TELEPATHIC MESSAGES

THE PERCEPTIONS WE RECEIVE AS WITNESSES to a ghost are projected by the mind of the apparition— telepathic messages. The witness perceives only what the apparition projects. So the clothing can change, as well as the form. Voices or smells or touches are perceived, but not actually physically sensed, which means that apparitions are telepathically spawned hallucinations—with a very intentional, though unusual, source.

We could say that we see an apparition because the apparition has psychokinetically played with our brain, causing the perceptual parts of the brain to assume that something was seen or heard or felt. Or we can say that the observer who has psychically picked up on the presence of the floating mind-without-body, telepathically reaches out to that mind to pick up enough information to create an image or sound.

In the case of the crisis apparition, we may be clairvoyantly or precognitively picking up on the death/dying process of the person seen.

CRISIS AND DEATHBED APPARITIONS

A FEW IDEAS HAVE BEEN PROPOSED about crisis and deathbed apparitions. One is that the appearance or dream of the apparition is purely coincidence and just a hallucination. Another is that the mind of the observer clairvoyantly or telepathically receives the information of the death and creates the hallucination to let the person know the event has happened—perhaps to lessen the blow of the more palpable news of the death when it comes in later.

A third idea is that the telepathic message is a deliberate attempt by the dying or just-dead person's mind to let people know about the death. The final interpretation is that the apparition, which may appear to more than one person—at the same time and even in different locations—represents the actual apparition, or ghost, of the person who just died and is dropping by to say farewell.

WORKS BOTH WAYS

REMEMBER, GHOSTS HAVE NO EYES TO SEE WITH, no ears to hear with. So just as the living need psi to perceive ghosts, the dead need psi to replace their lost physical senses. One would expect apparitions to perceive the world differently since their normal senses are gone and their minds must directly perceive the physical world. However, their own experiences and expectations may not be up to comprehending new perceptions, so that they still think of perception in the context of their lost senses.

Cases of communication with apparitions have not indicated that they have any special perceptions about the world. In addition, contrary to what some psychics and metaphysical practitioners say, the wisdom of the ages doesn't seem to instantly come to folks once they've died. To paraphrase Charles Tart, dying does not significantly improve our IQ. Just because they're dead doesn't mean they're smart.

It may be that apparitions, not knowing anything about psi while alive, don't understand their capability for enhanced perceptions after death. Possibly they can learn to use such new perceptual abilities. To my knowledge, there are as yet no cases of ghosts who have done so. On the other hand, some ghosts have certainly learned how to do PK.

APPARITIONAL PK

THE VERY DEFINITION OF APPARITIONS—minds without bodies—leads to an understanding that any physical interaction between such entities and the physical world is mind over matter. Ghosts move stuff by psychokinesis!

In fact, it is rare to find apparition cases where physical effects are occurring. Most apparition cases do not include unexplainable physical happenings of the type one sees in poltergeist cases. However, sometimes RSPK—recurrent spontaneous psychokinesis—develops in apparition cases. The fear caused by the encounters with the ghost creates enough stress that a poltergeist scenario also develops.

Physical effects in apparition cases tend to be minor. We see no big movements of objects, or things breaking, levitating, or acting up. With any genuine ghost photo or audio recording of spirit voices, PK would   be responsible. Follow me here, since this is   a   subtle aspect of ghostly inter-   actions.

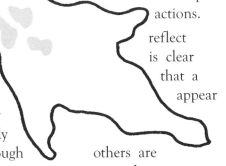

Ghosts don't   reflect light. That much   is clear simply considering   that a ghostly image may   appear on a photo—film or digital—taken by only one camera even though   others are being used at the exact same moment do not cap-ture the ghostly image. Just as a ghost would be telepathically interacting with you for you to visually perceive his form, the apparition might direct his intention at the camera to be "seen." Any intentional impact on the photo by a disembodied mind is PK.

Past parapsychological research has indicated that some living PK performers can affect film and even digital media. The living can do it, so we assume the dead can do it as well. That brings up a sticky point. It may be the photographer's PK that creates the image.

The expectation of people wanting to get ghost pictures may generate unconscious PK to affect the film or digital media. Or, as some researchers con-sider more likely, the telepathic connection between the apparition and the photographer causes the unconscious of the photographer to influence the photo being taken. It is even possible—though I have a hard time with this—that an apparition does not connect at all with the people present and only appears in a photo.

Close up of the Polaroid from earlier in the chapter. These light spots had no explanation, and corresponded to Annette's 'meeting' with the Blue Lady.

I receive many photos by mail and email with some kind of unusual images in them. People want to know if the anomalies represent ghosts. However, in most instances there was no other indication there was an apparition present, and often not even any past history of ghost sightings or hauntings in the location. It is certainly *possible* that an individual anomaly represents an apparition's attempt to be "seen" after being unable to otherwise communicate with the photographer. But without a human experience of a ghost or haunting to connect the anomaly to, it's more likely this is not the case, and the anomaly represents a photographic error and wishful thinking on the part of the photo-owners.

Ghostly Learning

IN THE RARE CASES WHERE THE GHOSTS are apparently capable of moving objects, there seems to be a pattern. First, these are longer-term situations, with the apparition being present for months or years before anything begins to move. Secondly, smaller things, then larger things begin to move. It is as if the apparition *learns* that she is capable of PK, and develops an understanding that as a being of pure mind, it is the mind that needs to connect with objects to get them to move.

What is interesting is that the movements are never as messy or energetic as in poltergeist cases. Apparitions are not subconsciously letting off steam in an uncontrolled fashion. They are trying to move things, presumably to get the living to notice their presence For an apparition, it is *all* about psi.

9

HAUNTINGS

AUNTINGS RELATE TO LOCATIONS, buildings, or objects. Something in the physical structure of matter records and holds bits of information that relates to happenings in and around the object, building, or location. Human beings, and presumably animals, can pick up this recorded information and process it in a way that allows them to perceive the content. Because the phenomenon often happens in a building or specific location, it's often called *place memory*. However, small objects such as pieces of furniture and even jewelry have been reported as being haunted.

Hauntings are experienced through the same range of perceptions as apparitional encounters. People see, hear, feel, and smell something not present in the physical environment.

Hauntings are a form of psychometry. The witness is "reading" bits of history from an object. In most cases the objects are big—houses, restaurants, hotels, or areas of land.

Many people look for ghosts in graveyards such as this one in Salem, Mass. But while hauntings can be perceived in such places, only rarely do ghosts hang out in cemeteries.

Researchers have found that people, who are unaware of the phenomena when they first walk in, are likely to perceive something in the same spots where phenomena were reported by the primary witnesses. This indicates that *something* in the environment at those spots exists on some level, physical or psychic.

REPETITION

UNLIKE APPARITIONAL ACTIVITY, what's reported in hauntings seems to be repetitive in nature. The same phenomena are experienced time and again by different people. The events played out seem to repeat themselves and human figures perceived seem to be without awareness.

The phenomena repeat in an apparent regular pattern. Often they can be connected to the timing of the original events. For example, footsteps that occur at 11 p.m. might be tied to that time because the prior owner used to pace up and down every night at 11. A murder that's perceived at 4 p.m. in the spot where it occurred years before is tied to that time because it happened at 4 p.m.

Sometimes hauntings are more active during certain weather or other environmental conditions. The haunt may be perceived when it's a dark and stormy night, the more electricity in the air the better. Or it may be tied to phases of the moon, or geological, geomagnetic, or sunspot activity.

EMOTIONS

EMOTIONS SEEM TO BE THE STRONGEST INDICATOR of a haunting. If you've felt good or bad vibrations or energy ever when walking into a building, even though you've never been there before, the feeling may be related to emotions imprinted in the environment in the past. Naturally, you would need to eliminate other possible causes for those emotional perceptions, such as décor, associations with the people present or who reside there, expectations about what's to happen in that place, and the emotional baggage you bring with you for that particular visit.

The content of haunting playbacks tends to be of emotionally packed events that people experienced in the past. Most hauntings reported have a negative emotion attached and may revolve around a murder, suicide, or beating. On the other hand, there are positive-content haunts. It is likely that people simply don't report hauntings whose content includes nice events or interactions. Most folks would take such perceptions in stride rather than seek help to rid themselves of the haunting.

Some hauntings revolve around nonevents. In other words, what's reported may be repetitive footsteps, pots and pans clanging in a kitchen, an individual walking up or down stairs or across a room, or other activities that would be normal for a living person

TIMES PAST

HAUNTINGS TYPICALLY REPRESENT RECORDINGS of events that happened sometime in the past. In older buildings, the haunt may center around events from dozens of years before, or even further back in time. In some cases, it's been interesting to figure out that the events imprinted actually happened on the land, either in a previous building on the property or simply on the bare land before the building was constructed.

In one of my cases, intense feelings of death and violence were experienced every few days in the kitchen area of the home.

A bit of research revealed that before the house was built there was a ranch encompassing the immediate neighborhood. The house was built approximately where the barn had been years before, and the kitchen sat on the spot where the ranchers had slaughtered cattle, pigs, and chickens.

The town of Tombstone, Arizona, is the site of many reported haunting imprints and apparitions.

YOUR OWN GHOST

HAUNTINGS CAN REVOLVE AROUND IMPRINTS of recent events. In one of my cases the "recording" was made only a short time before a couple moved into their house.

Because recent events can impact an environment, the figures perceived in a haunting can represent people still very much alive. Witnesses have seen apparitions of *themselves* in their homes, carrying out regular activities.

This intriguing phenomenon suggests that it's the living who impact the environment and are responsible for the activities and events that become haunting content. So we might well *imprint* the environment of the home while living in it and then *perceive* that place memory of ourselves!

If you think the sound of footsteps, or the figure of an old woman walking up and down the stairs—and vanishing—is scary, imagine seeing *yourself* as a ghost, or hearing *your* voice repeating something over and over. Weird, huh?

PERCEPTIONS

JUST AS PEOPLE ENCOUNTERING APPARITIONS may have different perceptual experiences of the ghost, people pick up hauntings in different ways. In contrast to apparitions, perceptions of a single haunting event do not vary as widely. Some people will pick up the phenomena the same way—hearing or seeing something—while others present will simply not perceive anything. If a young woman is repetitively seen walking the halls of a hotel, then vanishing, that's what most folks who are able to pick up anything perceive—those who are able to pick up anything at all. The story, what's reported to be happening, doesn't change, even over many years and many visitors.

The exception is that many people seem to be capable of only sensing or feeling something. So that when some might see the young woman's recording doing her repetitive walking, others may only feel something "weird" or "odd" or "strange" happening. Not everyone who enters a haunted house or other location experiences the events. Again, it may be that the sensitivity of certain people to these recordings is greater than for others, so the phenomenon may not be observed every time the physical conditions are met. Throw in the possible influences of mood and belief of the observers, and one may not get a thing.

The Bird Cage Theater in Tombstone. One feels the history walking through the place, yet something more is present.

Naturally, if the story of the haunting and what happens in the place is well known, suggestion probably is at play here. But it's interesting when folks who know nothing about the reputation of a place or specifics of a haunting, ask, "is this place haunted?" when they perceive things others have reported.

Duration

APPARITION CASES TEND TO BE OF SHORT DURATION, rarely going on for many years. Decades or centuries are even more rare. Poltergeist cases tend to last from a week to 18 months. Haunting cases may last as long as the building is standing, or even longer. In both apparition and poltergeist cases, the phenomena are dependent on people as the root cause—the living for poltergeists, the deceased for most apparitions. In poltergeist cases, the phenomena are physical for the most part, while in apparition and haunting cases they are perceptual. However, just as apparitions can apparently learn to move objects, there have been some reports of apparent poltergeist-like activity in haunting cases.

Psychokinetic Effects

THE EVENTS OF A HAUNTING SEEM INDEPENDENT of the people in the location. Like the other events reported in hauntings, the same kinds of physical activity happen over and over. The same kinds of things move regardless of who is present to witness, and regardless of how long the haunting goes on. The movements seem to connect to the original events that the haunt is replaying.

How a recording can cause things to move is a mystery unless we take one of two paths. First, there *could* be an apparition present. There are recorded cases in which an apparition stays with a location for years *and* there are place-memory replays that go on as well. In such cases, it doesn't take much reviewing of witness testimony and reports to determine that some of the events are connected to an interactive ghost and the others to repeating patterns. If objects are moving in cases with distinguishable apparitions, we can point to that entity as the likely cause of the physical happenings. The second path leads to psychokinetic effects caused by people in the haunted location. How that might work will be discussed in the next chapter.

Experiencing a haunting can bring up fear and other negative emotions and reactions—even more so when the content of the place memory is itself negative. However, keep in mind that a haunting is a *recording.* No consciousness, no malicious intent, no way to harm you—unless, as with apparition cases, your fear gets the best of you. Let's turn to ideas of how hauntings actually occur and whether there is a connection to psychic abilities.

10

HAUNTINGS AND PSI

F HAUNTINGS ARE BACKGROUND recordings that can be perceived, how does psi tie in? The haunting-psi connection is on the level of anomalous cognition—ESP except in cases where physical activities are also reported. People receive information from the environment. On the other hand, magnetic fields offer a non-psi explanation that may replace the ESP connection or may turn out to be part of the psi equation.

RECEIVING INFORMATION IN REAL TIME

PEOPLE DISPLAY THE CLAIRVOYANT ABILITY of psychometry—perceiving information associated with objects. In general, we think of a haunted house or piece of land as simply a big objects.

In the psi model of hauntings the specific local environment—the land the house is on and the house and its contents—holding the information of its history and inhabitants. We unconsciously scan it both with our normal senses and with psi and process the information received with emphasis on different perceptions. We use our psi to pick through the information recorded, and are more likely to notice the stronger imprints. Just as most people react to outside stimuli in similar ways, most people perceive the same bits of history.

Whether or not something dramatic occurred in a location, information charged with high emotion will be stronger and more evocative. Such emotionally charged imprinting, whether positive or negative, may catch our attention—just as a bright color or sharp noise is more likely to attract our attention.

While some believe that high emotion at the time of the original event "charges" the imprint is some hauntings seem to be fairly neutral in emotional content—such as the sounds of someone washing dishes. In a few rare hauntings, the imprint has nothing to do with people but with something that happened in the environment, such as a landslide, an earthquake, or an intense storm. Perhaps it was the emotions of those who witnessed events when

The Brook Room at the Brookdale Lodge, Felton, CA, has a whopper of an imprint: a huge party with a big band!

they occurred that imprinted the original recording. Environmental conditions at the time of the events being imprinted seem to be another factor influencing how some events are recorded.

In older locations, the disturbances reported may relate to different periods of time in the place's history. For example, a sense that violence occurred in the home may relate to prior owners fighting all the time, while footsteps heard on the stairs come from another inhabitant. A man seen carrying tools through the house may be an imprint of yet another time. Or all the events may relate to one set of past inhabitants.

As with apparition cases, different people may perceive the information of the haunt in different ways, with some hearing things, others feeling or seeing things. The variations are not as broad as in apparition cases, however. If footsteps are heard by a few people, it's likely that most who pick up anything psychically will "hear" footsteps. Some imprints seem to be stronger in the visual perception range, while others are more auditory or kinesthetic.

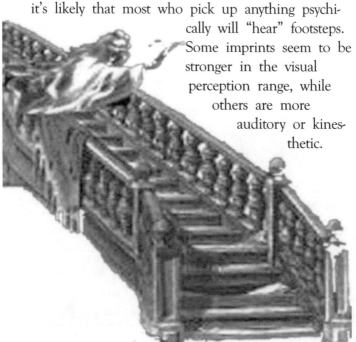

There may be a combination of perceptions, with the secondary perception being a feeling of something out of the ordinary. What's interesting is that while most people might not pick up anything visual or auditory about a haunt that displays such activity, they may feel something different in the spots where the haunting activity has been reported.

Sometimes a haunting does not relate to an entire house, but to a specific spot in the house. It may relate to a particular piece of furniture or jewelry. If an antique is haunted–filled with a strong imprint from the past–moving that antique around the house usually moves the haunting. It's like moving a portable stereo around–the music comes from the device.

RECEIVING INFORMATION FROM THE PAST

RETROCOGNITION, the ability to perceive information from the past offers another explanation for the psi connection in hauntings. People may pick up information directly from the past of the location or object, not from an imprint. Some people seem to be able to peer into the past for fleeting moments. However, the fact that unusual magnetic fields are often detected in the spots that are haunted indicates that retrocognition is not the explanation in most cases.

A sense of deja vu when entering a place may indicate a past life.

PAST LIFE MEMORIES

SOME PEOPLE REPORT A STRONG SENSE OF DÉJÀ VU—the feeling
of having been in a place in the past without actually
having been there—along with an emotional reaction to
some locations. Perhaps these people are recalling past life
memories—they lived there in a past life—rather than
experiencing an imprint of the past. However, this is
difficult to reconcile for most hauntings, since the haunting
activity seems independent of who visits.

THE MAGNETIC CONNECTION

USING MAGNETOMETERS, field investigators have found
something of a consistency from haunting to haunting. The magnetometers measure magnetic fields
given off by a variety of sources, both technological
devices and natural sources, including human beings
and the local magnetic field of the Earth. There is a
general background reading for any location. Readings

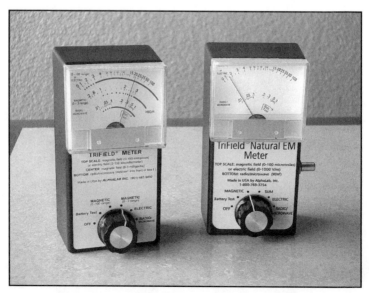

Two forms of magnetometers used in investigations.

increase when we bring a magnetometer near anything with a higher level of magnetic energy—such as
VCRs, digital alarm clocks, and electrical outlets.
Most magnetometers are set for the frequency range
of technology; while a few pick up the fields given
off by natural sources, including people.

What's so interesting in haunting cases is that
the spots where people experience the activity tend
to have higher than background magnetic readings—
sometimes much higher—even when all household
power is turned off. This effect has occurred in a
number of my cases. Sometimes we find a technological or natural source of the fields under or
outside the house, but it doesn't explain how the
field can be stationary and encompass only small
areas of the building.

Is the magnetic field indicative of the "recording"
itself? We're not sure yet, since the frequent use of
magnetometers in haunting cases began in the mid
1980s. Is the magnetic field an indication of something that *causes* an individual to be more psychic,
and so pick up the recording? Again, we're not sure,
but research by neuroscientist Michael Persinger and
others regarding the connections between the Earth's
magnetic field and humans' psi abilities, as well as
the use of such fields to cause people to have hallucinations, is particularly promising.

Psi and the Geomagnetic Field

Studies of the geomagnetic field in connection to
human behavior have been conducted since the latter
part of the 20th Century. Persinger proposed a couple
of possible connections with psi. One is that psi is
always working within us, but the geomagnetic field
affects the brain and its receptivity to the signals.

According to this theory, we are always being psychic, it's just that only under certain environmental conditions can we consciously receive, process, or even remember the psychic information. Given other recent environmentally connected findings, which I'll discuss in a later chapter, it's likely that psi is influenced by some combination of factors.

Another view is that geomagnetic fields somehow affect the incidence of psychic experience, allowing them, or even causing them, to happen. Pursuit of this theory has led to findings that intense magnetic fields can actually cause hallucinations. Persinger has developed the means to bombard a subject's brain with such intense fields as can be found in real life, and has learned that subjects will experience hallucinations of varying types, including some that are similar to NDEs, apparitional encounters, and even alien abduction scenarios.

SKEPTICS

CALLING ON THE HALLUCINATORY EFFECT of magnetic fields, skeptics assert that hauntings are merely the result of the brain reacting to these fields. However, what's *missing* in the skeptics' model is how the hallucinations include factual historical information. How is it that a person can have a vision of the murder being committed when they have no knowledge of the location's history or of the murder if it is merely a hallucination caused by magnetic impact on the temporal lobes of the brain?

I see no basic conflict here. It may be that instead of psi operating, it is some kind of magnetic perception. We simply have not figured out the piece that provides information within the hallucination as yet. Research along these lines is likely to pay off soon. Imagine if we could control the incidence of historical hallucinations. We might be able to find a way to bring out imprinted information anywhere for anyone. Imagine visiting any historical site and being able to perceive events that happened there.

WHAT IS THE RECORDING MECHANISM?

WE ARE NOT CLEAR ABOUT WHAT ACTUALLY RECORDS the information. Any discussion of the process is speculative at best right now. It would appear that the information has some connection to magnetic fields. Research has confirmed the potential for utilizing magnetic fields to record information—that happens with audio- and videotape, for example. In light of Persinger's work, it may be that the information is

The Australian aborigines have a long tradition of connecting to the Earth and the ancestor spirits.

both recorded and played back through our brains with some magnetic interactions. Or it may be that the magnetic fields simply cause our brains to be receptive, while information is recorded in some other fashion.

HAUNTINGS AND PK

THERE ARE RARE OCCASIONS IN WHICH PHYSICAL objects move in hauntings. Parapsychologists generally believe that PK activity in a haunting results from people in the haunt at the time. This may be tough to accept, since I have already stated that hauntings can take place over decades or centuries, which does not explain how a living poltergeist agent for movements occurring over hundreds of years.

The model, sometimes called *haunting RSPK* (recurrent spontaneous psychokinesis), says the activity is the result of the imprinted information received by the people at the haunted location or object. Most of us are capable of unconsciously creating PK, with our

stresses and moods, that can impact on machines and computers. In haunting RSPK, visitors to the haunted place pick up information subconsciously, which their minds may process into the perception of the imprinted events. In some people, this barrage of information sets off a burst of subconscious PK, which is directed by the "story" being perceived. Because the imprint doesn't change much over the years, different visitors become agents of the same haunting RSPK effects. In other words, our subconscious mind, picking up even more than our conscious mind, helps the story along because of our expectation of what occurs in ghost cases. By *expecting* more to happen, we make more happen.

In some haunting cases, the PK-related activity seems to be random, having no connection to the replayed events. Generally, such activity is limited to a single set of inhabitants and doesn't reoccur over the years. It's thought that the haunting causes enough stress that one or more of the folks living there become poltergeist agents as a result of experiencing the place memory, especially when the recorded events are of negative emotional or violent content.

11

POLTERGEISTS

HE TERM *POLTERGEIST*, coined centuries ago in Germany, means *noisy ghost*. The phenomena associated with poltergeist scenarios are centered around physical events that make noise, throw things, knock things over, and generally cause havoc. Often referred to as "mischievous spirits," poltergeists exhibit intention behind the activity, which can lead to the conclusion that there is one or more invisible entity acting behind the unusual activity.

Questions regarding these mischievous spirits kept coming up throughout the 19th and 20th centuries. Events appeared closely tied to living were present when things happened. Since the mid-20th Century, the current model of the poltergeist has held sway, owing largely to the work of parapsychologist William G. Roll. This model looks to the psychokinesis of a living agent, not a ghost, though in rare cases an apparition might be responsible for PK effects. The range of effects has changed, even expanded, perhaps because of the "stuff" we have around us. In fact, many poltergeist scenarios revolve around technology of one sort or another—something not dealt with until relatively recently.

The author prepares for a poltergeist investigation.

RELEASING STRESS

ROLL'S RSPK (RECURRENT SPONTANEOUS PSYCHOKINESIS) model points to unconscious of a living person experiencing stress as the causative agent. The poltergeist is an example of mind over matter gone haywire so that hidden stresses and pent-up emotions of the agent release his bottled-up feelings outward.

People have quite a range of ways to release tension, emotion, and stress. Some use meditation, some use physical activity, some use creative arts—often with impact on one's own body. Stress may cause illness, sometimes seriously. Not everyone, however, knows how to meditate or has beneficial ways to blow off steam. People may express pent-up emotions verbally, even physically by lashing out at others or objects. For some people the release of stress is unseen—except for the effect around them.

Have you ever been so stressed out or frustrated that you just wanted to hit something? Hopefully, you didn't act on this impulse except perhaps with a punching bag. Keeping such agitation bottled up can be hazardous to physical, psychological, and emotional health. Some people release intense feelings through PK.

Unconsciously blowing off steam through PK gets blame placed on the perpetrator. In fact, a poltergeist agent rarely suspects that she is responsible for the chaotic happenings when things get broken or malfunction—a ghost is blamed instead.

People very rarely get hurt in poltergeist events, unless they forget the cardinal rule here: never ever duck *into* the path of a flying object! When they do get hurt, it's typically the poltergeist agent himself who experiences the physical "attacks". In one of my cases, a woman experienced having attacks on her throat nearly every day. Her throat bulged out and marks began to appear on the skin. Looking at the attacks, how and when they started, and what was going on in the woman's life led us to a startling conclusion. She had been struggling with intense guilt because she had finally spoken out about being abused as a child by her late father. The attacks, which were directed at her throat—actually the area of her larynx—stopped when she understood that her unconscious was trying to get her to "shut up."

Hauntings and Poltergeists

Visual Effects and Archetypes

Poltergeist cases have, on rare occasion, provided visual apparitions, though these are generally distorted, archetypal, or even monstrous. In these cases we don't get a basic human ghost, but a projection of stress, guilt, anger, fear, or frustration from the subconscious—a projection that the agent is telepathically sending out to others in the household.

In my very first case, a family reported PK activity and seeing a knight in black armor and seeing. The black knight was conceptually connected to the 16-year-old boy in the household, who hardly lived at home, owing to delinquent activities that had landed him in hot water. Through the investigation it became clear the boy's mother was the poltergeist agent, and the black knight was a projection of her intense but unconscious desire to blame his bad behavior on an evil supernatural entity. The black knight was quite archetypal. There's a reason Darth Vader looks the way he does in the *Star Wars* series.

Setting and Duration

Typically poltergeist cases are of limited duration, only a couple of weeks to about 18 months. This contrasts with apparition cases, which vary dramatically in the duration; and hauntings, which are related to the actual location and may last for many years, even centuries.

Poltergeists can usually happen within family settings, although there have also been poltergeist cases investigated in workplaces. The activity and the stress behind the poltergeist may be specific to one person or may be related to the family—or work group—interactions. As a result, in some cases it would appear that there is no one poltergeist agent, but a group source of the PK. Even in cases with a single agent, it may be that the pattern of activity begins when a certain combination of family members is present with the agent.

Unlike hauntings and most apparition cases, poltergeists can follow people from place to place. Naturally, if a *person* is the cause, wherever that person goes, the poltergeist goes—so long as the stressors that caused the RSPK continue.

Adolescents

THE GENERAL STEREOTYPE of the poltergeist agent has been popularized by the press and the film industry—as well as a few horror writers—as a teenage girl. In reality, the RSPK can occur with agents of either sex and just about any age above 10 years old. One reason teenagers have been labeled is that most poltergeist cases do indeed occur with agents in their adolescent years. Adolescents have inherent stresses on the body and mind The start of puberty is not the same for all kids and adolescence does not end merely because an individual turns 21. For some, the growing process continues well into the twenties.

Identifying the Agent

THE POLTERGEIST AGENT CAN generally be pegged by looking for patterns of activity and who's at the center of those patterns. The objects affected may belong to one individual in the household, or be representative of a role of one member of the family.

Often the physical things affected in a poltergeist case can be used as clues to determine what's bothering the poltergeist agent.

SYMBOLISM

IN SOME INSTANCES, the events that happen are symbolic of the deep issues causing stress. When unusual events occur, it can be helpful to look at the objects or events as metaphors much as we analyze objects from dreams. Bursts of water may be symbolic of tears of grief or sadness, or to a specific happening in the life of the agent—such as a fear of swimming or a lashing back at parents forcing a child to be on the swim team. Fires sometimes break out in poltergeist cases, and usually indicate intense anger. Unlike in the movies, the fires are tiny and generally leave a burn mark on furniture no larger than the burn of a cigarette. Blazes only break out in horror films. and books

CATCHING THE PETULANT CHILD

IN POLTERGEIST SCENARIOS, the subconscious mind "plays" like a petulant child, throwing things around and affecting things in disturbing ways. There is little danger of reprisal because there is no reason to point a finger of blame at the agent. Like a child, the poltergeist agent's mind stops the happenings when "caught"—when the agent is forced to confront the reality of being the root cause of the occurrences.

The PK phenomenon *itself* can be an intense stress-point that helps escalate the RSPK. In other words, a little PK causes the people, especially the agent, to stress further, causing more unconscious PK. Having the phenomena stop at the point of accusation and acceptance may actually be more than simply the unconscious poltergeist feeling caught. Fear of psychokinesis is common. The idea that our thoughts can manifest in physical actions—and the responsibility that brings—is very scary indeed. The RSPK may simply turn off at the point of revelation because the agent now, consciously, must accept the PK as coming from herself.

If the agent does not deal with the root causes, stress and what's causing it, the RSPK may reoccur. Sometimes poltergeist agents accept the PK as their own and seem to gain control of the psychokinetic ability so that the PK is minimized to small object movements or minor effects on technology. The concept of PK seems to bring limits of belief. It's hard for most people to accept that their *unconscious* minds can toss things through the air.

BRAIN ACTIVITY

STRESSES ARE NOT THE ONLY POSSIBLE CAUSES in RSPK cases. There may be a neurological explanation. In groups of poltergeist agents given neurological examinations, there were signs of epilepsy and epileptic-like activity in the brain in a significant percentage of the agents. In one group 33 percent exhibited some epilepsy-like activity. A hypothesis put forward is that for *some* people the RSPK may simply be another form of epileptic seizure. In some cases where such activity was found in the brain, agents felt "better" or "relieved" after an RSPK attack.

FRAUDULENT PK

GHOST HUNTERS SOMETIMES ENCOUNTER fraudulent PK. In the typical poltergeist case, most families do not know how to pin down what is going on. So an unseen—and generally "evil"—unknown entity is often blamed for the happenings. An emotionally disturbed person in that situation may actually have created a pseudo-poltergeist on his own, purposely moving objects through purely physical means to lash out at the family.

There are situations in which the conscious mind imitated the unconscious PK. If the subconscious mind does these things to let off steam without incurring blame—"the ghost did it!"—the conscious mind could certainly recognize such possibilities. Ghost hunters must watch out for both real and pseudo-poltergeist activity.

12

POLTERGEISTS
AND PSI

OLTERGEISTS ARE IRREVOCABLY TIED into psi. Movement of objects and other physical effects caused by a mind—conscious or unconscious, living or dead—are by definition psychokinesis. Poltergeist activity, even if caused by mischievous spirits, would still be PK-related. As we have seen, parapsychologists relate this activity to living people.

PK AT A DISTANCE

THE POLTERGEIST AGENT IS USUALLY PRESENT in a location when activity happens. There are instances, however, where a later-identified agent was in another room and sometimes out of visual range of the activity's central points. In rare cases, the agent wasn't even in the building and may have been miles away, but the agent's thoughts were focused on that location.

In such situations, the question is how the unconscious mind knows what to throw around. Perhaps the PK force involved simply knocks over or
throws things at random. Although in many poltergeist cases, there's a clear connection between the
affected objects and the agent, so random action
seems unlikely. Generally, the agent knows the activity center well, so it may be that his memory of
where things are allows the PK force to affect the
right objects.

On the other hand, perhaps some form of clairvoyance—of anomalous cognition—is involved. PK
doesn't seem to have a problem working interactions
with technology, effects on very small physical processes and pieces of matter, and psychic healing. PK
seems to work whether or not the PK agent is aware
of the target's structure, or whether she is aware of
what needs to be affected to make something happen. Apparently the part of the mind tied to PK
performance simply *knows* what to affect.

All current evidence points to some kind of
receptive psi process that directs the PK force.
Whether in an intentional PK experimental task or a
poltergeist scenario, information inexplicably combines
with PK to make sure the right things happen.

BELIEF AND LIMITS

PK RESEARCH INDICATES THAT PK performance is tied
to belief. The PK performer's general beliefs about
psi and psychokinesis are particularly important.
Experiments with believers and disbelievers, have
shown that those who believe psi may exist out
perform disbelievers. Belief in the possibility of psi
seems to provide safe ground for someone to be a
bit psychic.

The Banta Inn near Tracy, CA. is home to a ghost who loves moving objects around in full view of customers and employees.

With PK performance, as with athletic performance, belief seems to be the all-important factor. It's difficult to do something when you don't believe you can. Believing in the possibility of PK at least opens the door for you to experience it. There are levels of belief.

Believing in PK does not mean that we believe we can do PK ourselves. Accepting the possibility that "I can do psychokinesis" increases one's potential to do so. Accepting as a reality that everyone can do PK, "myself included," increases that potential even more so. Belief also affects how much PK we can do—how big an object we can move, for example—and what kind of activity we can do—such as healing, movement of objects, effects on technology, and metal bending. Often we humans set our own limits.

ACCEPTING RESPONSIBILITY

PEOPLE TEND TO SIDESTEP ACCEPTING RESPONSIBILITY for all of their actions. The very idea that our thoughts—especially our uncontrolled thoughts—can be directly turned into action can be frightening. PK is a scary thing for most people.

RSPK gets around issues of belief and acceptance of personal responsibility because the subconscious mind is responsible for the poltergeist's messy activity. The subconscious is disconnected from our conscious beliefs in limitations and the fears and doubts triggered by the idea of being able to do psychokinesis. This is the reason PK activity tends to stop when a poltergeist agent accepts the fact that he is personally responsible. The fears and limitations we consciously set as part of his personal belief system snaps back in place, and the poltergeist goes away.

People who have turned the subconscious poltergeist experience into a conscious PK ability typically accept PK as real and accept the ability as real for themselves. They typically accept PK as a positive rather than negative skill. They divorce their emotions from the ability, so when they want to do PK it's something interesting to do, rather than something that causes them emotional upset.

The author with Banta Inn owner Joan Borland, one of the main witnesses to the ghost's appearances and antics.

Psi Stress

STRESS IS USUALLY AT THE ROOT of the poltergeist
phenomenon. On rare occasions, the stress the agent
feels comes not from normal activities and interactions, but from psychic ones. Having repeated psychic
experiences such as precognitive dreams can be
emotionally distressed. People living in the middle of
a haunting, or in a home that has an active apparition, are usually distressed and afraid. Occasionally
the stresses of such experiences cause someone to
become a poltergeist agent—which then causes more
activity and more stress.

It is important to consider psi as a source of
stress when other causes for that stress can not be
identified. Ghost hunters should avoid discussing this
possibility possibility unless the circumstances suggest
such a possibility, which may cause even more stress,
and thusly escalate the activity.

Apparitions as Poltergeists

IN SOME RARE POLTERGEIST CASES, people have seen
apparitional forms. Apparitions seem to be able to
learn to do PK in some cases. How can we determine if an apparition is causing the activity? How
can we determine if the apparition is genuinely there
or is simply a projection of the mind of the agent?

Some poltergeist cases could be caused by an
invisible entity. In the late 1970s, British parapsychologists Alan Gauld and A. D. (Tony) Cornell put
together criteria to help distinguish between poltergeist activity caused by the living and such activity
caused by unseen agencies, though they admitted
their criteria are a bit "crude."

How to Determine When Psi Activity is Caused by an Unseen Agency Rather Than a Living Agent

First, occurrences in the poltergeist case seem unrelated to any one person's presence or may seem to transfer from centering around one person's presence to that of another.

Second, the apparent purposes of the incidents seem unrelated and perhaps even contrary to the motivations of those living in the situation and their pattern of interrelationships.

Third, there are several sightings or several simultaneous witnesses of the appearance of an apparitional figure or some misty shapes that appear to be initiating the activity or may be directly related to the phenomena.

Fourth, the sum of the individual incidents appears to far exceed what we consider the capacities of psychokinesis or the phenomena occur in ways that seem to be at odds with the poltergeist agency being a living person

The presence of these circumstances would point us in the direction of an apparition. There are potential problems with some of these criteria given what we do and don't know about psi, so we need to be flexible and adapt to the specifics of each case.

CAVEATS TO THE GAULD CORNELL CRITERIA

IT IS POSSIBLE THAT AT TIMES THE AGENT does not need to be physically in the setting. A stressed agent away from home thinking about home might cause some minor events to happen. In such cases the phenomena may depend not on whether the agent is *physically* present but on her *psychological* proximity. But in almost all cases, the presence of the agent seems to be necessary for phenomena to be considered a genuine poltergeist. If this factor is missing, we might lean toward the apparitional interpretation.

Occasionally, a haunting might include spontaneous psychokinetic activity without any evidence of a ghost. Since a haunting is a psychic recording picked up by visitors to a location, it may be that the recording can set off a visitor's PK, thereby causing the occurrences to repeat with various sensitive visitors or "temporary agents". Because all visitors to the haunted location may be potential temporary agents, the absence of an identifiable living agent is not necessarily a point in favor of the apparition hypothesis—we could be dealing with neither a poltergeist nor an apparition.

Psychic Aiko Gibo talking with a little girl's apparition in an old house in central Florida.

When investigating poltergeist situations we must be careful to not jump to quick conclusions. These cases often involve very intricate psychological sets. The investigator needs to dig deeply into the dynamics of the situation to determine if there are *hidden* stresses that could cause the "contrary" pattern.

TELEPATHIC HALLUCINATION

IN SOME CASES OF APPARITIONS seen in poltergeist cases the living agent has apparently created apparitional figures that were seen on more than one occasion by more than one person.

The figures represented demonic or mythological figures, or something entirely from the imagination, such the knight in black armor that one of my clients family's experienced. In these situations, the most likely paranormal scenario is that of a living poltergeist agent calling up and projecting images from his subconscious. We would call such a projection a *telepathic hallucination*. The agent's mind creates the image—a hallucination, since it is imaginary—which is broadcasted to others. Some would perceive the figure and others don't, just as with an actual deceased entity.

One real indicator for me is the appearance of an apparitional figure. Frequently a telepathic hallucination does not look like a person, and instead symbolizes the fears of the agent or represents some mythic entity she can blame the activity upon.

BIGGER PHENOMENA

THOUGH FLYING OBJECTS SEEM TO CONTINUE to be the common feature, the activity has moved from feces—yes, that's right—in early cases, to rocks pelting houses, to weird behavior of appliances and electronic devices.

More physical events happen in poltergeist cases than in apparitional ones. Bigger things move, which may indicate that we living folks have that much more psi power than ghosts have, or that apparitions aren't skilled in using their PK potential.

The explanation that the incidents are contradictory to other living-agent cases is a variation of the happenstance of too much PK for the average poltergeist, which may be the strongest indicator of an outside agency's being the cause. Taken separately, these criteria are more or less "crude," as Gauld and Cornell say. But, if there is a combination of factors, it may be just as likely that the agent is a deceased entity as a living one.

DURATION

THERE IS ONE MORE DIFFERENCE between poltergeist and apparition cases—duration. The phenomena associated with an apparition's presence may continue over many years or even decades, through a succession of different people living in the location. Poltergeist cases tend to be short lived, almost always less than two years and generally only lasting a few weeks. If an apparition hangs around for a while, the PK may not even begin until months or years after the ghost is seen, and may continue for as long as he is around.

13

CONTROVERSY

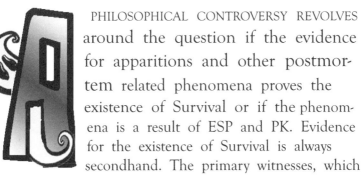PHILOSOPHICAL CONTROVERSY REVOLVES around the question if the evidence for apparitions and other postmortem related phenomena proves the existence of Survival or if the phenomena is a result of ESP and PK. Evidence for the existence of Survival is always secondhand. The primary witnesses, which are the apparitions themselves, cannot be objectively detected as of yet—at least, not with any reliability. Apparitional experience, whether your own or that coming through a medium or channel, can be looked at in one of three ways.

First, there's the possibility of being mistaken, that what is seen or experienced is not what is actually going on. This interpretation is the easiest to deal with, as we can usually get a good idea whether the processes going on are normal rather than paranormal. Second, we could say that the evidence may actually support after-death existence. However, there's a third possibility that makes all the difference—your own psi abilities may be responsible for the experience.

These questions have been at the center of a major philosophical debate for decades. One side favors the Survival hypothesis, while the other side points to the psychic ability—a "super-psi" or "super-ESP"—of the living as being responsible for creating the sense that a discarnate entity is around.

Eileen Garrett, mid-20th Century medium who founded the Parapsychology Foundation.

MEDIUMSHIP

MEDIUMSHIP PROVIDES an example of the conceptual problems. Communication between a medium and a spirit requires an information exchange using psi. As discussed earlier, communication between apparitions and living people takes place through a telepathic pathway. This posed a problem for early researchers, namely that the medium may be picking up the information from the minds of the living people. The medium may receive information via telepathy or even clairvoyance—psychometry—and not from an apparition at all. To deal with this confusion the medium's mind simulates an apparition as the source of the information and the "spirit" is essentially window dressing.

To control for this possibility psychical researchers worked with proxy sitters. The medium contacted the deceased person in the presence of the proxy who was an uninformed stand-in. The proxy then took the information relayed

Eileen Garrett's ability impressed even tough researchers.

by the medium back to the person whose relative was contacted for verification. Still there's still the psi problem. Because the limits of psi are unknown, it was theorized that the medium's psychic abilities may have enabled him to locate the real sitter to pick up information from the mind of the sitter or from existing records about the deceased person to be contacted—a sort of a remote viewing of an individual.

The dilemma was that if the information that verified the apparition's message existed—whether in someone's mind or in physical records—the medium may have used telepathy or clairvoyance to access it rather than actually getting it from a ghost. Yet, the medium's belief system would lead him to conclude that he had received it from a discarnate being.

APPARITION AS HOLOGRAM

THE APPARITION AS A HOLOGRAM is a super-psi theory that postulates that apparitions are not conscious and are not the minds of deceased people, but are creations of the mind of the observer. Most apparitions hang out in locations where they lived, worked, or played. If it's true that the environment locks in information throughout the history of the location, then the apparition may merely be our mind's version of a hologram from something akin to the *Star Trek* holodeck—a room that allows infinite hologram simulations of people and places. The mind

The USS Hornet in Alameda, home to dozens of apparitions.

receives information about a person from the past of that location, which it uses to create a simulation of that person to communicate with.

Unlike a typical haunting, in such instances, for some unknown reason, the "ghost" can enter into communication with the witness—because it is the mind of the witness that actually pulls the holographic puppet's strings. Perhaps the reason more than one person can experience the interaction at the same time is that the imprint of this person has more detail than in typical hauntings. Apparent movements of objects relating to the ghost is PK, as with haunting cases that have physical object movement.

INTERACTIVE HALLUCINATIONS

ANOTHER VIEW IS that the apparition case relies on the living witnesses to create the entity. Other witnesses who experience the same thing at the same time do so because their own psi enables them to pick up the projected apparition-hallucination from other witnesses. Alternatively, it may be that the "program" that is the imprint is a matrix of information that leads to the same experiences.

Bob Rogers in the corridor above the stairs to the engineering area of the USS Hornet where he saw an apparition of a chief petty officer.

Psi-generated apparitions have accompanied more than one poltergeist experience. In such cases the ghost is usually not human or representative of anyone who lived. The difference may be a result of the source of the information. In a poltergeist case, the apparition is generated from the subconscious of the agent. In the holographic haunting model of apparitions, the information comes into the witness's subconscious from the imprinted environment and is formed into an interactive hallucination.

APPARITIONS AS DISCARNATE ENTITY

THERE ARE SEVERAL POINTS in favor of apparitions being discarnate entities. First, the degree of interaction can be high. It is simpler to imagine this happening with conscious entities. The communication and content of communication between apparition and observers can vary dramatically over time. People living with ghosts have reported different conversations with the apparitions each time they encounter them, even though witnesses of an individual conversation can all report the same flow of information.

The concept of super-psi applied in apparition cases is overly complex and misses some crucial components. For example, while there are cases of hauntings caused by imprints of living people, the apparitions of living people experienced behave differently from the apparitions of the dead. We would expect at least some holographic haunting cases to include living people as the subject of the apparition, but such cases have not been reported.

The apparition of a man in khaki uniform appeared on these stairs to the engineering bay on the USS Hornet.

An additional point is that some apparitions are of people who had never visited the location in life. The ghost interacts and may communicate verifiable information. Generally there is an acknowledgment that he had never been to the house or building before. If the individual had never been in the place, the concept of any sort of imprint, complex or otherwise, flies out the window. It's simpler to look at interactive apparitions as simply that: conscious entities without physical bodies.

Until we know the limits of what a living person can do with psychic abilities, consciously or unconsciously, or perhaps until science can determine if the brain can generate a consciousness that is separable from the body—any evidence for survival can only be suggestive. It is very strongly suggestive mind you, but suggestive nonetheless.

Psychic Stache Margaret Murray assisted my investigation of the USS Hornet.

To paraphrase Gertrude Schmeidler, it may be that we will never know if we are wrong. If there is life after death, then all the indications have been right on target, and we'll find that out when we die that we still have an existence. If there is not existence after death, we would not know anything when we die.

14

NOT PSI

ARAPSYCHOLOGY INVESTIGATES phenomena unexplained by known laws of science. When we develop an explanation that science can accept, parapsychologists must redefine the field or walk away. I prefer the former. Parapsychologists study psi experiences, including apparitions, hauntings, and poltergeists by examining at all sides of the experience. Only by eliminating the natural or normal explanations can we study what doesn't fit.

Intense Magnetic Fields

THE WORK OF neuroscientist Michael Persinger in Canada shed light on the connection between psychic phenomena and the Earth's magnetic field—the geomagnetic field. The geomagnetic field is generated as the planet, which is thought to be liquid at the core, spins. It has both global and local components and can be affected by solar activity and tidal forces from the moon. On a local level, Earth movement in and around fault lines, can impact the field.

Persinger's work indicated that local fields can impact psi as well as a number of kinds of brain activity. He utilized artificially created magnetic fields of the same frequency and varying intensities as the geomagnetic field. He showed that with appropriate intensity, the field can cause an unusual form of activity in the temporal lobes of the brain, which is correlated with unusual experiences.

Persinger created a helmet that simulates intense geomagnetic fields. Subjects reported vivid, seemingly real hallucinations that are similar to alien abduction experiences, NDEs, apparitions, and the kinds of things people report in hauntings. Such intense fields can occur naturally. Indeed, ghost hunters using magnetic field detectors have found such fields present in apparition and haunting cases.

This may be an explanation for apparitions and hauntings at least for some experiences. There are a couple of missing pieces, however. For one, the kind of verifiable information that often comes through in apparition and haunting cases is missing in the magnetically induced hallucinations. That many

Photo by Dave Manganelli.

These mysterious orbs of light were created by a camera flash reflecting off crumpled aluminum foil, just below the frame.

people experience the same thing over long periods of time, indicates that there's much more to this than magnetic fields simply causing hallucinations.

JURY STILL OUT

IN A CASE reported by William Roll and Andrew Nichols, a haunted bedroom showed unusually high fields on the geomagnetic frequency. However, a room on the other side of the bedroom wall showed no such field. More importantly, the room directly below the bedroom in question also showed no intense field. The frequency was akin to the geomagnetic, but it was not a geomagnetic field.

In one of my apparition cases, a couple reported interacting with the ghost of a young woman. While a colleague and I were there, they both saw her appear in the living room. Our instruments detected an unusually high magnetic field at the spot where the ghost was seen, but it was yards away from the people experiencing the apparition. The couple de-

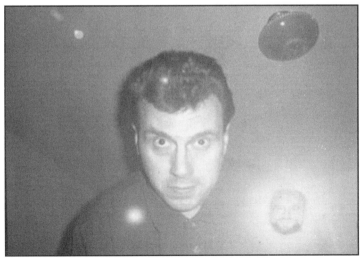

Investigator Dave Manganelli with a few 'spirit orbs,' including one that resembles the author. Created with simple photo software.

scribed the ghost walking across the room and we were able to use our magnetometers to follow along where they pointed, as the magnetic field became mobile. This is not the behavior of a typical natural geomagnetic field. The explanation that "it's just from intense magnetic fields" is insufficient. Whatever is going on, this is pretty cool stuff!

PHANTOMS ON THE BRAIN

AT THE TURN OF the 21st Century, Peter Brugger, a neuroscientist in Zurich, proposed a new explanation for ghosts, OBEs and NDEs. For years Brugger's had researched how the brain creates the sensation of phantom limbs—sensations in an arm or leg that persist after the actual arm or leg has been amputated. Brugger postulated that OBEs and doppelganger sightings—seeing one's own ghost—may be a brain activity similar to what occurs with phantom limbs. By extension, this explanation can be applied to apparitional and haunting experiences.

Brugger's explanation may hold some water in explaining bilocation people certain OBEs, as well as experiences where see themselves from outside their bodies or as apparitions or doppelgangers. OBEs often occur between wakefulness and sleep. While there is altered brain activity, it is unclear if this validates Brugger's explanation. Brugger's theory also fails to explain situations where the person in the OB state is capable of "traveling" to another location and return with verifiable information.

PHANTOMS OF THE EYES

BRITISH SCIENTIST Dr. Dominic FFytche has advanced another explanation for ghosts. His explanation is rooted in the phenomenon of deterioration of vision, which can occur on a temporary basis for people with good eyesight. He found that people with degenerating vision sometimes report strange hallucinations under certain conditions, often on the order of distorted faces.

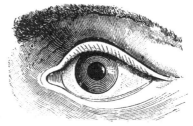

Ffytche's theory might explain some small portion of ghost cases, where the figure is seen as distorted and not heard, felt, or smelled. But the majority of apparitional experiences involve clear visions of the ghost and/or voices, scents, or feelings coming from outside the witness' body.

PHANTOMS OF SOUND

SOUND MAY BE RESPONSIBLE for what we feel in hauntings and the things we might see. In the late 1990s, Vic Tandy, an expert in computer-assisted learning at Coventry University in England, experienced the effects of a haunting while sitting in a medical laboratory in a building he'd been told was haunted. He experienced discomfort, then a cold chill and felt depressed as he sensed something else in the room, and the feeling that he was being watched. Then he noticed something out of the corner of his eyes which became a human figure. It was shadowy and not clear. Tandy gathered his things and left the building, a normal reaction for most people in such a circumstance.

The next morning when reflecting upon the odd experience the glimmerings of an explanation began to emerge, though the explanation itself seemed out of some fiction.

Tandy, who was a fencer, had one of his swords in a vice for modification. Realizing he needed some oil, he left it there and headed out on a search. On his return, he noticed that the end of the blade was vibrating intensely and realized the cause of the vibrations might be low frequency sounds in the building.

Most people know that high frequency sounds—ultrasonic—are inaudible to humans. However, our hearing also has a lower threshold. Infrasonic sounds are those below that threshold. The cause of these sound waves can range from machinery and other technology to power lines and even earth activity.

Tests were conducted that revealed the existence of a standing sound wave of low frequency bouncing around the lab, reaching its highest intensity next to where Tandy had been working when he saw the apparition. The sound wave was apparently caused by a new fan making the air vibrate at a par-ticular rate. The ghost and the sound wave departed when the fan's mounting was altered.

Interestingly, the sound wave was at approximately the same frequency as that determined by prior research to cause a resonance vibration in the human eyeball. Think of how your body vibrates when you're near a blasting stereo with the bass turned way up. While not infrasonic, bass is lower frequency. Different parts of our bodies vibrate in sympathy with different low frequencies. When a sound wave makes the eyeball vibrate, shadows and other indistinct forms may appear in the periphery of your vision.

This explanation is another piece to the massive puzzle of what's behind apparition and haunting experiences. Naturally, infrasound is an explanation to be applied to haunting cases, since the sound-created experiences don't include interaction as with apparitions.

PHANTOMS OF SLEEP

AN EXPERIENCE connected to all three ghostly situations is the often-reported "I woke up in the middle of the night feeling someone or something was sitting on my chest." Called the "old hag" phenomenon in past ages, this experience has a reasonable explanation.

The graveyard in Salem, Mass., where the dead have not been seen to rise.

Many people experience "sleep paralysis" when in the dreaming state. When we dream of running or engaging in another physical activity, the nerves involved in that activity when awake are firing, but our bodies are effectively paralyzed, preventing us from acting out the impulses from the firing neurons. That's a good thing, by the way.

You have probably has the experience of waking up from a dream to find your arm flopping around, eventually coming awake with that pins and needles feeling. This is a result of lingering partial sleep paralysis. This can happen with your legs or even your torso. The people experience of "someone is sitting on me" is caused by a part of the body being in the sleep paralysis state.

When it happens to people sleeping in a house reportedly haunted or visited by an apparition, their minds attribute ghostly phenomena as being the cause of the experience. However, people experience this all the time in non-ghostly locations and never look to ghosts as the cause. Some people with particular religious beliefs *may* believe it's a demon—but that's a different discussion altogether.

JUMPING TO THE WRONG CONCLUSIONS

SKEPTICS AND DEBUNKERS seize upon nonpsychic explanations such as those discussed. It is amusing—and nonscientific—that the disbelievers use such explanations to explain away *all* apparition, haunting, and poltergeist experiences.

It's nonscientific for informed skeptics—many of them scientists—to use Persinger's magnetically induced hallucination explanation or the infrasound explanation to imply that skeptics formulated the explanations and spread the word. Persinger's discoveries grew out of cooperation with parapsychologists. Tandy's article on infrasound and hauntings was first published in the *Journal of the Society for Psychical Research.*

Parapsychologists formulated many of the nonpsychic explanations.. After all, we're trying to figure out what's really going on. To do that, we have to eliminate nonpsychic explanations, so we continue looking for new ones. Of course, nonpsychic explanations should always be considered. Many reports of apparitions, hauntings, and unusual things experienced in poltergeist cases have nonpsychic explanations. But missing pieces from these explanations indicate that something more *is* going on. This is what parapsychologists and professional ghost hunters are studying. It is disappointing that so few scientists look into these experiences. Their input could help further our understanding of other nonpsychic explanations and speed up the process of understanding what the experiences represent.

People often ask me if nonpsychic explanations are disheartening, given that I am trying to find evidence *for* ghosts. On the contrary, I am encouraged that another piece in the puzzle of human perception is revealing itself. The more it is that we expand our perceptual abilities beyond the traditional senses, the closer it is that we get to understanding psi, which appears to be the perceptual path for interaction with discarnate entities.

15

THE CASE OF LOIS

HE CALL CAME FROM A WOMAN named Pat in Livermore, California, a city east of San Francisco. Pat was an attorney who lived with her son and husband. She said she was prompted to call because her son had been having conversations with the ghost of her house's previous owner—and that these almost-daily conversations had been going on for well over a year. The call was intriguing and begged to be followed up upon.

Pat's attitude was refreshing, as was her story. She and her husband had purchased the 70-plus-year-old home in an estate sale a couple of years after the previous owner's death by natural causes. The woman had lived in the house from her birth in 1917 until her death in 1980. Since moving into the house, Pat, her husband, her mother, who lived nearby, and her son had seen the apparition of a woman appearing and disappearing in the house.

Pat indicated that she had grown up in a family environment that acknowledged psychic experience, so she was not afraid of the ghost. Still, she hadn't shared her experience with the other family members

until her son spoke up. Her mother and husband
had also seen the ghost, but had kept the sightings
to themselves.

One day, Pat's twelve-year-old son Chris began
talking about the origins of the antique furniture
and porcelain dolls that had been purchased with
the house when they bought it. Pat asked her son if
he had found some kind of paperwork about the
items, replied matter of factly, "Lois told me." Lois
was the name of the late owner.

After Chris's revelation, Pat spoke
with her husband and mother, who
admitted that they, too, had seen the
ghost on several occasions. But it was
to Chris that Lois showed herself
every day. Apparently she felt
most comfortable around him.

Pat had some concerns about
having a ghost in the house
with a growing almost-teen. By the
time of her call, she had taken her
son in to see a psychological counselor to make sure he was "okay"
and that conversing with the ghost would not be
damaging to him.

I had lunch with the counselor who had seen
the boy. While he admitted to being a bit of an
agnostic when it came to ghosts, he was convinced
that Chris was well adjusted and not prone to making things up, consciously or otherwise.

Pat said that Chris got verifiable information
from Lois. This is a rarity when it comes to apparition cases. I was excited about the case and agreed
to an on-site meeting with Pat and her family.

FEAR OF BLASTERS

PAT SHARED A CONCERN of Lois's about my visit, which she told Chris, and he told his mother. Apparently, Lois watched television quite a bit with Chris and had seen a commercial for the movie *Ghostbusters*. She told Chris that she was worried that I'd bring along "blasters" to get rid of her. I assured Pat that I had no such equipment.

CONVERSATION IN THE CAR

A FRIEND, Joanna Rix, along with one of the transpersonal counseling students, Kip Leyser, accompanied me on the field visit. As we drove from JFK University to Pat's home, which took a little less than an hour, we talked about a number of things— some of which came back later to "haunt" us. The car I was driving was giving me problems and I talked about my desire to buy a new car. Joanna mentioned her concerns about work and that she was contemplating quitting her job that week. Kip surprised us by revealing that he had been a professional dancer for ten years before coming to JFK University.

We arrived and were greeted by Pat, her mother, and Chris. Pat's husband was out of town at the time. As we were invited in, I got the impression Chris seemed to be giving us the visual once-over to make sure we had no ghost traps. We started a tape recorder and walked around the house, discussing the various sightings of the ghost that they had had.

Different Appearances

PAT AND HER MOTHER had briefly seen the ghost on a few occasions. She always appeared to them as an elderly woman. Chris had been seeing Lois almost every day for more than a year. He said she didn't always appear as an old woman to him and that sometimes she often looked like a teenager, sometimes like a six-year-old, sometimes like a woman in her thirties, and sometimes a middle-aged woman.

"Does her clothing change often?" I asked. "All the time," he replied.

Pat and her mother also remembered seeing Lois wearing different clothing. That she appeared at different ages in different clothing was important.

I asked Chris how that was possible. He said that Lois told him that she believed she did not have a "form." She told him that she believed she was some kind of "ball of energy" that was able to communicate by "projecting her thoughts" to others. These thoughts included visual and verbal information that she "projected into the minds of others" so they could "see" and "hear" her as if she were really there. Remember, this report came from a 12-year-old.

Chris' report indicated that Lois was aware that she was "telling" Chris's mind what to "see" and "hear" about her. They were not actually seeing and hearing Lois with their senses, but that. they were *perceiving* her—and both Lois and Chris were aware of this.

"Why is Lois appearing in different forms and clothing?" I asked. "Because that's how she feels each day," he replied.

What Chris' report shows is that it was Lois's own sense of self, her perceptions about the way she viewed herself that day—at a particular age in particular clothing—that shaped her "projection" of herself.

INTERVIEWING LOIS

WE FINISHED TOURING THE HOUSE, hearing about some of Lois's furniture and her doll collection, about the city of Livermore, and about Lois herself when she was alive. For a twelve-year-old, Chris was an amazingly articulate purveyor of anecdote. In fact, I had little trouble believing that Lois was feeding him the information.

When we returned to the living room, I asked if we could ask Lois some questions. We sat down facing Chris, who was seated next to an empty chair that he identified as Lois's favorite spot to sit. According to the boy, she was sitting there with us.

The three of us pitched questions at an empty chair as a young boy looked and listened to "someone" sitting there, repeating or translating "her" answers. There was a surreal feel to the situation, as if we were in some weird situation comedy. While Joanna and Kip asked questions more related to Lois herself, I kept to questions related to her current incarnation as an apparition.

The answers were specific and to the point. More and more information came out about Lois, giving us the picture that she had been a social butterfly, often hosting parties at her home throughout her life. Most of her relatives had died, but she spoke of one who was still alive.

For me, Lois described, through Chris's excellent translation, her form and her ability to communicate on a telepathic level with Chris. She declined to appear to us, however. She said she didn't quite trust us and admitted she wasn't even sure she ever would. She speculated that the family being able to see her might have to do with their attachment to the house and with how psychic they were.

Most of what Chris said Lois told him about her form as an apparition familiar from my readings in professional parapsychological literature—not from popular books about ghostly phenomena. This was a surprise coming from a twelve-year-old boy who, according to his mother, had never read anything on ghosts.

Fear of Hell

I ASKED LOIS WHY she had not passed on and was still hanging around her old house. The answer was that she had done much socializing, had many parties in her life, and had not been an avid churchgoer. A believer in heaven and hell, she thought too much partying and not enough church might see her to hell, so she figured it was safer to stick around rather than take the chance of ending up in hell. Besides, she told us, she liked the new family and felt very happy with them, especially Chris.

We cannot conclude that there is a heaven or hell form Lois's comments, only that Lois believed there was. We can infer, however, that her belief and her desire to stay in her house somehow enabled her to stay as an apparition. It would be a mistake to generalize from this that such a desire can enable others to remain as ghosts, since environmental and some person-specific factors were probably in operation that allowed Lois to stay. Otherwise, we would have many more apparition cases than we do.

LOIS SHOWS OFF

I ASKED IF Lois had questions for us. Lois decided to show off. Chris looked to the empty chair and then asked us each a question.

"Loyd, she wants to know if you've decided on a color for that new car you want to buy". "Joanna, have you really thought about the kind of job you want after you quit the one you have? "Kip, how long were you a professional dancer?"

Our three jaws probably hit the floor at the same time. In hollow voices, we each answered Lois' questions. Then after explaining to Pat and the others that the questions related to our in-transit conversation, I asked how Lois knew to even ask the questions.

Chris looked over to the chair, then back at us a bit sheepishly. "You're probably not going to like this, but Lois wanted to make sure you weren't bringing blasters to get rid of her, so she hitched a ride with you on the way here. She heard everything."

We all laughed nervously. Kip was especially shaken, since the only place Lois could have "sat" was next to him in the back seat. We got up to leave, promising continued contact and follow-up.

Verifying the Story

BACK AT THE OFFICE we reviewed the tapes listening for any indication that we had somehow told the family about our conversation in the car. We concluded that either Chris—or Lois—read our minds, or that my car was bugged, or that Lois really had caught a ride with us. To this day, I'm sorry it didn't occur to me to ask how Lois got to JFKU to get into my car in the first place. Did she hitchhike there? Take a bus? Fly?

Subsequently I located Lois's only living relative. The elderly gentleman, who was able to verify the tales of Lois's youth as true, as well as information that Chris had relayed about the family and Lois's house. In case you're wondering, Pat thoroughly checked to see if Chris had found diaries or other papers Lois might have left behind. None could be found.

Chris continued to see Lois on a daily basis for a while, but then lost some interest as he moved into puberty and discovered real girls. According to Pat, Lois is still in the house, is still seen on occasion by members of the family—and is still happy to be in her lifetime home. Lois showed herself to be a person first, and a ghost second. She proved my adage that "Ghosts are people, too."

This case is my favorite for many reasons. First, the verified information was sufficient to convince me that normal sources of information could be ruled out. Lois was there or perhaps Chris was some kind of super-psychic who was able to pick up the information from the house itself through clairvoyance or retrocognition. That there were other witnesses to Lois puts heavier emphasis on the former possibility rather than the latter.

Second, the information about how Lois was able to appear and communicate was far beyond what most people would have been able to read about easily at the time, let alone the kind of information that a twelve-year-old would spout about ghosts.

Third, the fact that the family called us in because they, too, were curious about apparitions was refreshing and enabled us to ask the kinds of questions I wanted about the how and why of apparitions.

Finally, the fact that the family was well-adjusted, seemingly without psychological issues about the ghost, was encouraging because so often the first impulse people when they see a ghost is to turn and run

16

THE SEXORCISTS CASE

AN ODD HAUNTING I investigated while in New York shows that, contrary to popular belief, hauntings don't always emanate from evil or negative events in a home. Actually, the opposite is often true. A friend from my college days, Judy Cole, who was writing for *Playgirl* gave this case—and me—the title "The Sexorcist."

Fresh out of grad school, I had been working for a short time at the American Society for Psychical Research in New York City. Part of my job was to answer calls from people who thought they had encountered ghosts and such.

I got a call from a man who had moved into a five-year-old home in upper Westchester County with his wife about three months earlier. They called about a "problem" they were having. It seemed that nearly every night around three a.m. they were awakened by what sounded like two people in the next bedroom. -

I asked, "What kinds of sounds?" "Sounds," he said hesitantly. Again, I asked, "What kinds of

sounds?" The caller replied in the same hesitant way
and I asking the same question again. Eventually he
gave more detail:

The caller replied, "Noises ... sounds ... of two
people ... ah, you know ..." Again I asked, "What
kinds of sounds?" The caller replied, "You know,
sounds two people make."

"What kinds of sounds?" I asked emphatically.
"Sounds of two people ... doing it!!!" he finally
blurted.

As the caller and his wife were the only people
living in the house, they thought maybe some spirits
were making whoopee. This wasn't a problem except
that the sounds were so loud that they woke them
every night.

Every night at three a.m., with the exception of
Sunday night into Monday morning, they were awakened by loud moans, grunts, and even screams—of
the less painful sort, fortunately. One or both of
them would get out of bed, leave their room, and
go into the hallway to listen. The sounds continued
until one of them crossed the threshold of the
second bedroom, at which point the
sounds stopped. Then they
could go back to
sleep.

There was no
other sign that the
place was haunted,
just the apparently
sexual antics of
an invisible couple.

"Are you fright-
ened?" I asked. "No,

just really annoyed," said the caller. "And we're tired from being woken up every night and to be honest, tired from not going back to sleep because we're trying to figure out what they are doing when they make all that noise."

I scheduled a visit for a few days later. In the meantime, it was fairly clear to me what was probably going on. This was probably not two ghosts having astral sex, but a haunting. The repetitive pattern was a dead giveaway. Also, there were no indications that ghosts, ones with intelligence, were involved. However, it was not a negative haunting, even though it was annoying to the people living there. Some people might have been entertained and even turned on by such a haunt.

My investigation of the property indicated that it was part of a new development in a wooded area, that no other structure had been at the site, that there were no historical events that would impact it, and that it was not a Native American burial site. In fact, it was clear that no one had had any real problems in the immediate area, including deaths. Only one other couple had lived in the house previously and had lived there for nearly the whole five years of the house's existence.

My visit turned up nothing in and around the house indicating anything out of the ordinary. That is often the case with hauntings, as one may have to be around at the time of the pattern's replay to pick up anything weird happening.

The couple and I walked around the streets of the neighborhood. They told neighbors we encountered that I was there to investigate a haunting. But they were too embarrassed to say how the haunt played out, so we were a bit vague about the phenomena. The neighbors were surprised to hear that the place might be haunted, given that it was a very subdued area. Nothing seemed to happen in this neighborhood.

The key finally came from a next-door neighbor who told me about the previous owners, a couple who were alive, well, and living in Manhattan. This neighbor had been one of the first into the development and pretty much knew everyone.

This is my recollection of what he said, not exact wording. He said, "Yeah, they were a nice young couple. They had just gotten married before moving in. We liked them a lot, but I did have one complaint about them." He looked a bit sheepish when I asked him to go on. "Well, they used to wake us up every night around three in the morning."

"How?" I probed. "Well, during the spring and fall when we didn't need either heat or air conditioning and windows were left open, we could hear something from their house. They used to make the loudest noises when they were going at it. Having sex, I mean. Right there in that bedroom closest to our house." He pointed at the bedroom from which the haunting sounds were coming.

My Conclusion

THIS PREVIOUS COUPLE MUST HAVE MADE LOVE with such emotion that they impressed it upon the environment and the new dwellers were psychically picking up on it. In other words, the previous owners had left a really good impression behind.

The next step was to give some advice to the couple about how to deal with the annoying phenomena. Getting rid of a haunting can be easy or difficult; it's not like you can simply switch it off. So I offered the couple the following options:

Ignore it and you'll eventually get used to it, like getting used to road noise when you live next to a highway. Their response: "Could *you* get used to that?"

Record over it by having some big party in your house, lots of noise, and center it in that room. Their response: "Could that mean we would then be woken up by sounds of a party every night?"

Go in there and record over it by making love in the same room at three a.m. Their response: "We'll think about it."

These days we have other methods of dealing with hauntings, including involving psychics or magnetic fields. But at the time, without a psychic, these were the best options.

I left, planning to speak with them a few days later. In the meantime, having gotten the phone number of the prior owners from the next-door neighbor, I gave them a call. They were quite surprised to hear that the place was haunted, and couldn't understand how that could be.

"What does three a.m. mean to you?" I asked. There was silence. Finally, the man said, "Why do you ask?" I explained what the phenomena actually were. More silence.

"Well, I can't exactly say why, but yes," said the man, "at three a.m. we'd get up and make love." "And Sunday night to Monday morning?" I asked. "After a lot of weekend partying, we needed to get a full night's sleep."

As for the haunted couple, which option do you think they chose? A few days later, they called to tell me they'd chosen the third suggestion. They liked the idea so much that they moved their bed in there, and set their alarm for three a.m. Now the only sounds they heard in that room were their own.

But one has to wonder about the next people to move into the house.

17

Two Poltergeists

URE POLTERGEIST CASES are few and far between. The PK phenomena rarely escalates to a level where there's a need for a site visit. Actually poltergeist cases can often be handled over the phone. Naturally, this depends on how much activity there has been and how frightened the people are who experience it. But here are two cases that illustrate the classic RSPK (recurrent spontaneous psychokinesis) scenario.

Appliance Hell

ON ONE OF MY TRIPS back to New York to visit family, I was referred a case near my parents' home. A woman in her late twenties had had a baby several months before. She and her husband were living in an apartment that seemed like the least likely place for anything ghostly to happen. However, quite suddenly the electric appliances, TV and stereo had begun acting oddly.

According to the woman—we'll call her Jane—the TV changed channels by itself, turned itself on and off, and the volume often cut out. The stereo came

on by itself, or if running already, suddenly turned
off. She told me that most of the unusual activity
happened in the kitchen area. Appliances on the
counter came on by themselves, or turned themselves
off mysteriously when already running.

They had checked the electrical system for power
surges, but nothing indicated any electrical problems.
They had "tried to ignore it until stuff started flying
around the kitchen," she said.

What prompted Jane to call was that plates and
glassware in moved the cabinets, glasses slide across
the counters, and plates banged up and down on
the table. Given that the area was not prone to
earthquakes and that they were not on a well-traveled
street—the rumbling of big trucks can cause a building to shake—they had concluded "something paranormal is going on."

I drove up to the apartment and met with Jane,
who was still on leave from work and home taking
care of the baby. Her husband was at work and
unable to join us.

As we walked around the apartment, I could not
see anything that would fall into the "normal" expla-

nation category to
account for the re-
ported events. If the
electrical system was
fine—I checked this
with the building
manager and it was—
then the behavior of
the appliances was
hard to explain. One
could, of course, say it
was just a series of

individual malfunctions that coincidentally happened around the same time, but given the list of phenomena she reported, that was highly unlikely. The situation was especially strange in light of the fact that several of the appliances had gone on without being plugged in!

Naturally, they could have made all this up, but having personally seen such phenomena, I was inclined to try to help them.

EXPLORING STRESSORS

PUTTING ON MY PARAPSYCHOLOGIST HAT, I asked Jane questions about when the events happened, who was in what room, and what they were doing at the time. I also asked about what stresses they may have had and if the stresses were shared or individual.

Very quickly, the picture formed of what was happening. Jane was on maternity leave for several months, much longer than they had anticipated when arranging for child-care. They were having difficulty figuring out the child-care situation, as it

Ashley's Restaurant, Rockledge, FL., where science fiction writer Martin Caidin took the author and a team to investigate apparitional sightings and strange movements of objects.

was too expensive for them. Jane's husband continued to bring up the suggestion that she leave work to stay home to take care of the baby—at least for a couple of years. Jane liked her job and was anxious to get back to work. She loved being with the baby but was bored. She said she felt "stressed out with all the boredom."

Jane and her husband argued frequently about her going back to work. The arguments clearly put a strain on their relationship. Jane felt resentful of her husband's being able to come and go as he pleased—though she admitted this was mainly to and from work. She was angry that he expected her to *want* to stay at home to cook and keep house for him and the baby. She was angry that her husband just

wanted her to be a housewife permanently. She rejected the whole idea.

The TV's behavior seemed to center around times when her husband was watching sports and "acting like a typical male." This seemed to be the most likely time that volume cut out, the uncontrolled channel surfing happened, or the TV would turn itself off altogether.

The appliances started acting strangely when Jane began feeling resentful about "being stuck in the kitchen." Regardless of where in the kitchen they were standing, whenever they were in the kitchen arguing something on the counter turned on and off. As the arguments progressed, the events spread beyond the appliances to glasses and dishes. Sometimes the events occurred when her husband called home from work and an argument ensued.

I explained the poltergeist scenario, about PK and its link to stress. I pointed out that Jane was the likely RSPK agent in this case, and that her stress was what was causing all the happenings. I added that it was the interaction between herself and her husband that was at the root of the PK-causing stress.

Jane actually seemed relieved, as she admitted to having fantasies of angry ghosts or demons, and was afraid for her baby. She promised to sit down with her husband to discuss the root causes and to seek couples' counseling to resolve their differences.

In a follow-up call, I learned that all was calm. In fact, between their discussions and brief therapy sessions, her husband agreed it was better for her to go back to work than for them to have a poltergeist in their home. Jane added an amusing point. Too bad they couldn't control the effects. After all, having appliances run without electricity could have saved them a bundle of money!

The apparition of a man has been reported as seen in the area below the dining balcony of Ashley's Restaurant.

The Crying Ghost

Not all poltergeist cases exhibit object movement or revolve around the emotions normally considered stress-related. Sometimes sadness is the catalyst.

I received a call from a family who reported bursts of water in their home that had no apparent cause. The bursts were sudden and often large. The couple claimed that they and their granddaughter were drenched by these strange events. They reported that clothing in drawers and closets got soaked, even though it had been dry moments before. The phenomena had been going on for some time.

When I visited the house, several things quickly revealed what was happening. The couple was older. Their 14-year-old granddaughter was living with them because her parents had died in an automobile accident over a year before. She seemed emotionally withdrawn, almost emotionless in her responses to our questions.

Moving through the house and seeing the water damage to the walls and furniture was interesting, as it had no boundaries. The water-bursts happened all over the house, even in the girl's room.

From descriptions of the events, it appeared that the girl was always present in the room, whether one

or both—or neither— of the grandparents were there. The first of the indoor storms happened less than a day after the anniversary of her parents' death.

A GOOD LONG CRY

A MEMBER OF THE INVESTIGATION TEAM asked a couple of telling questions. Had the girl processed her grief? Had she been to see anyone for counseling after the accident. The answer was "No. In fact," noted the couple, "we can't even recall her crying at all."

The girl was quite attentive, though still expressionless as we discussed what poltergeists represent. We discussed approaching the events in a poltergeist case the way one would the elements of a dream. In a dream analysis, one might say the water bursts represented the repressed tears of grief the girl was holding inside. In order for the phenomena to stop, she needed to express her grief in normal ways—to have a good long cry. She needed to confront her feelings of grief and loss about her parents.

The grandparents promised to get her into grief counseling. We recommended a couple of therapists and departed. I later learned that the young girl began crying the moment after we left, her tears continuing through the night. The water bursts never occurred again.

*The brook running through the Brook Room of the Brookdale Lodge, Felton,
CA. A little girl, who fell and died decades ago, still visits the Lodge.*

18

WEIRD
NOT PARANORMAL

ASES THAT COME TO ME often have circumstances that lead people to mistakenly believe something para-normal is happening. Sometimes it is because of simple suggestion coupled with a willingness or even desire to believe. Other times there may be explanations that are unusual, or outside of the average person's experience, knowl-edge, and expectations. Unfortunately they are often told by non-parapsychologically friendly resources to "see a psychiatrist," which could result in their being diagnosed with some kind of dysfunction rather than getting an explanation for the odd experience. Here are a couple of examples of the unusual, though "normal" variety.

NUTTY GHOST IN THE ATTIC

DURING MY DAYS at the American Society for Parapsy-chological Research (ASPR) in New York, I investi-gated a case in a heavily wooded area of the suburbs northwest of Manhattan. The couple reported hearing the sounds of footsteps, which were loud enough to record on tape, in their attic every night around 11 p.m. When they went up to the attic to investigate, no one would be there and they could find nothing that could have caused the sounds. The footsteps were irregular, not like someone was pacing, but like someone crossing from one side of the attic to the other.

I arranged to visit the house and to spend some time in the attic around 11 p.m. Stakeouts are common in a ghost hunter's line of work—although we do try to avoid waiting on phenomena that might not happen. That's to be done first. In this case however, there I was, the intrepid ghost hunter, preparing to stake out the attic—alone.

Just before 11 p.m. I made myself comfortable on the bumpy rough-hewn wood floor of the attic. The ceiling was only about five feet high at the center peak. I hunkered down with a flashlight in hand, ready to shed light on whatever might appear and stomp around. There I sat alone in the dark.

Confronting the Ghost

I REPEATEDLY CHECKED my watch's luminous dial. Shortly after 11 p.m. I heard scratching sounds, but I couldn't tell where they were coming from. Then silence, as though whatever it was was waiting for a sign that all was clear. *I held my breath.*

After few more scratching sounds, I heard light thumping sounds. Straining in the dark to hear exactly where the sounds emanated from, I realized that the thumps were coming closer and closer to me.

When the thumps were only a few feet away, I aimed my flashlight at the spot where the thumps were loudest and turned on the light and ... saw the face of an incredibly shocked squirrel pushing some chestnuts across the floor of the attic.

The squirrel—who was just being a squirrel—must have been terrified by the ghostly light beaming on him, because he turned tail and sped out of there. I laughed, switched on the attic light, looked in the direction the squirrel was headed, and traced his path to find his way in and out. I had been sitting almost on top of his stash of nuts, which explained why he had come in my direction.

I picked up a few of the chestnuts and rolled them one at a time across the floor, watching as each one bounced over the bumps in the wood. While the immediate sound of the nuts bouncing wasn't very loud, it apparently reverberated in the space below the attic floor, echoing enough to sound like the footsteps that scared the inhabitants.

"We hear it!" shouted the man on the floor below. "What do you see?" I rolled another nut, and got the same response, though this time they added "Loyd, are you all right?"

I snagged a bunch of the chestnuts, shouted "Yes, I'm fine," then tossed the handful across the floor. The couple screamed as the acoustics made the bouncing nuts sound like the attic had been invaded by an army of ghosts.

I went down out of the attic to gave my clients a full explanation. It took awhile for them to accept it. I had to perform a demonstration for them separately with one up in the attic and the other one downstairs while nuts were bounced across the floor. The next day the hole was sealed and another ghostly threat was squirreled away!

Eco Haunting

FRIGHTENED PEOPLE can suffer psychologically and physically in certain situations without a bit of psychic phenomena taking place. Getting professional help can be difficult because what's happening to them seems straight out of a horror movie. I was called in on such a case in the San Francisco Bay Area city of Martinez, California.

The affected family was renting a relatively new home. The four of them had been experiencing dizzy spells in specific spots in the house and they periodically suffered from sudden, intense headaches. They regularly smelled foul odors that had no apparent cause and often felt their hair standing on end. They saw fireballs, which left scorch marks on walls, counters, and even furniture mysteriously appear in and around the house. They thought they were under attack and worried that the house was haunted. They wanted to move out but their landlord would not release them from the lease.

They called a local university and were politely told they should seek serious psychological help. They spoke to a local skeptics group and got the same unhelpful advice. Something about their claims, notably that there were four witnesses, caused my team to visit the house.

Upon arrival at the house, we noticed right off that it had been built right below high-tension power lines. Whipping out our electromagnetic field meters, we measured extremely high fields, as expected in such a situation. The power lines gave off an audible hum, a constant annoying sound. We suspected that we would find inaudible low frequency sounds as well.

We were given a tour of the long ranch-style home. Family members showed us damage from the fireballs and pointed to where they smelled the noxious odors. The investigating team members felt dizzy in a couple of spots in the home and began to develop headaches when we stood in those spots. We examined the house, considering what nonparanormal factors could account for what the family was experiencing, and our own reactions. As we gathered meter recordings and antidotal evidence we began to account for the various physical and psychological experiences and reactions the family had reported.

NOT A NORMAL HOUSE

THE HOUSE HAD SHIFTED slightly off its foundation, to the point where the floors were not level. Doors and window frames were not 90 degrees, especially in those areas of the home where dizziness was prevalent. When we expect things to be square and they are not, human perceptual processes play tricks on use to make things neat. Our life experience has conditioned us toward comfort with right angles. Slight deviations from right angles, while generally unnoticed by the conscious mind, can cause people to experience dizziness and headaches. The continuous low background audible hum of the power lines could contribute to causing headaches.

Low frequency sounds can affect emotions. When the frequency of the sound is in a certain range, the fluid in the eyeballs can be affected and shadows might be "seen" out of the corner of the eyes. While we didn't have the proper equipment to detect such sound waves, given the experiences reported it was likely the power lines were giving off low frequency sound.

There has been much speculation—and some legal cases—surrounding high electromagnetic frequencies from power lines affecting people's health. While the jury is still out on what kind of impact such electromagnetic fields have on our health, we do know that high magnetic fields can affect the brain and perceptual processes to produce hallucinations.

Using a very low-tech detector we recorded lots of static electricity in the house,. Waving around a fluorescent light tube through excess static charges will cause it to light up—and ours did. That accounted for the hair-on-end-experiences that the family reported.

The investigating team experienced the noxious smell the family had reported. Inspecting the parameter of the property, we noticed that the house was on the other side of a hill from a landfill. The noxious smell was methane, likely seeping up through the ground from the landfill. The fireballs? The pockets of methane could have been ignited by the static charges in the dry air.

The house was an environmental nightmare, not a paranormal one. Some one from the investigative team who was familiar with local zoning ordinances, gave the family good information that enabled them to get out of the lease.

Having so many different nonparanormal explanations was quite eye-opening. It underscored that we must always look deeply into any case, taking the events and experiences one at a time as well as looking at the overall situation. Such cases demonstrate the need for understanding how and why people might come to the conclusion that their house is haunted.

Only by thoroughly investigating the location in Martinez, looking for alternative explanations to "it's haunted" and "they're crazy" could anyone come to the conclusions we did. Otherwise, the family would have continued to get reactions from the professionals they sought help form that they were just another crazy bunch of people. It is rarely as simple as "they're imagining things."

19

Ghost Hunting Tips

ORE AND MORE PEOPLE are interested in ghost hunting. If you want to become a ghost hunter, consider what kind of ghost hunter you want to be. There's a lot of good and bad information on the Internet and on TV, which is where most people tend to get their education on the subject. Investigating reports of ghostly phenomena can be easy or hard, depending on the case and on the investigative goals.

Many amateur ghost hunters, relying on misguided sources, head for spooky old buildings and cemeteries and gather pictures and recordings that fail to prove anything. They have gotten their "proof" at locations that had no actual incidences of apparitions or hauntings. There are a few ghost encounters on record in graveyards, but they are few and far between. Hey, if you were a ghost, would *you* hang out in a cemetery?

Such amateurs miss the most exciting parts of investigating: the experiences of witnesses—the ghost *story*—and the potential to have one's own experience. They often overlook the mystery to be solved.

If you want to be more than a thrill-seeker, then read what you can about parapsychology, psychic abilities, and the research and investigation of others. This book is only a beginning. I've included a short bibliography at the end for further reading, which will take you to more sources. My Web site, listed at the end of this book, has ever-expanding bibliographies and ever-updated lists of resources for good information on the paranormal.

Be discerning when researching the topic on-line. Too many people claim all sorts of things that range from misinforming to wacky to downright harmful. When you are unsure about a perspective or "fact," compare it to source material from mainstream parapsychologists.

Question claims that a source individual is a parapsychologist to begin with, since so many make this claim without having any idea what a parapsychologist actually is. Some of the worst offenders are psychics who for some reason think that being psychic allows them to call themselves parapsychologists. This mislabeling is like any of us calling ourselves "psychologists" since, after all, we have minds don't we?

Some so-called parapsychologists have gotten a "degree" from diploma mills on the Internet, a less-than-academic mail-order program, or from some wacky certification from people who are not qualified to give out certifications. Check their credentials,

OFFICE OF PARANORMAL INVESTIGATIONS

especially if they claim to have a Ph.D. in parapsychology. Only a couple of individuals in existence have such degrees from accredited universities.

Ask lots of questions and consult sources like the Parapsychological Association, the SPR, the Rhine Research Center, the ASPR, or the Parapsychology Foundation. Links to those organizations can be found on my Web site, or by simply running a search through Google or one of the other search engines.

If you haven't done so already, pick up my book *Ghost Hunting: How to Investigate the Paranormal*, for a more detailed manual on being an effective paranormal investigator. Here are a few dos and don't's for investigating cases of apparent apparition, haunting, or poltergeist phenomena.

GHOST HUNTING DOS

Do learn the basics of what parapsychologists and psychical researchers have learned about apparitions, hauntings, and poltergeists, even beyond what you've read here. While some amateurs dismiss parapsychologists and their literature, there is quite a lot to learn—as I hope you've seen in this book.

Do learn about psychic experience and abilities. The basic model of ghosts requires that some form of psychic communication and perception be happening. Hauntings, too, seem to rely on some form of receptive psi. Poltergeist cases—and any ghost cases involving physical effects—cry out for an understanding of PK.

Ignoring what has been learned in parapsychology can mean wasting time rediscovering what is already known or could mean heading down the path of misunderstanding.

Do learn the concepts of physics before believing pronouncements about other dimensions or parallel universes, including proof of other dimensions from which beings can cross into ours. Nothing of the sort has been proven. A basic conceptual understanding of physics helps to sort through the morass of bad information presented as fact.

Do learn about the uses of technology in an investigation. Learn how to actually use the technology that ghost hunters use. Learn what the devices are *designed* to detect—it's not ghosts—and learn the technology's limitations.

Take the time to think through what the readings, photos, and recordings actually represent. Just because you have an anomalous something, don't leap to the conclusion that it's a spirit or something from another dimensional plane.

Do develop interviewing skills so that you can question the witnesses appropriately. The very definition of apparitions and hauntings requires the *experience* and *observation* of the phenomena by a human being. Focus your attention on the perceptions and experiences of the witnesses in the situation. Getting useful information from witnesses requires the best interviewing skills you can develop.

Do look for nonparanormal explanations for the
overall case you investigate *and* the individual
events reported by the witnesses. Question
everything. Observe thoroughly. Cases are rarely
so cut and dried that everything reported or
experienced is paranormal or normal. Often
the witnesses are so freaked out by an encounter that they become suggestible or
misinterpret normal noises and movements in
their homes that they hadn't noticed before.

*Do realize that some explanations can be rather bizarre
without being paranormal.* Look for unusual and
rarely seen normal explanations. Read up on
such unusual explanations. Old and new
unusual explanations should be considered,
such as the hallucinogenic effect of magnetic
fields on the brain and the uneasy feelings
and peripheral images caused by low frequency sound. The more you know about
what it isn't, the better you are at determining what it might be.

Do take note of people's experiences and perceptions.
Work with psychics or sensitives who are
team players and willing to be questioned
about what they experience. Work with
psychics who can accept that they are not
always right and who are willing to dissect
their perceptions. It doesn't hurt to ask the
if they can perceive any nonparanormal
causes.

Do pay attention to what you experience yourself.
Always look for alternative explanations.
Consider your expectations. If you get too
caught up in your own experience, especially

if you desire to encounter something psychic or spiritual, you may find yourself misinterpreting what's really going on. Take your perceptions apart and do not immediately label a perception or experience.

Do take special note of instances when both the technology and the humans are sensing something out of the ordinary at the same time. Technology can support the experiences of the witnesses and psychics, as you look for correlations between unusual readings, photos, and recordings and the anomalous experiences of people.

Do combine all data from technology with the experiential reports of the witnesses and any perceptions of sensitives, your teammates, and yourself before making a final judgment of what's going on and how much is or isn't paranormal.

Do realize that cases can be mixed. I've investigated cases that had combinations of hauntings and an apparition, sometimes related to each other. I've had poltergeist cases in which the stress that caused the PK was in turn caused by the experience of a haunting or an encounter with an apparition. I recently had a case in which an apparition was visiting in a house that also had a pretty strong imprint of a past inhabitant, causing lots of stress and leading to some RSPK activity.

Do respect the people in the location you investigate. Cases involving private homes usually revolve around the family's need to get rid of the phenomena. If you are called in to help, do not leave without providing them

some kind of assistance, even if it is only
referrals to other qualified specialists. Spend
time educating the family about psychic
experience and apparitions, hauntings, and
poltergeists. Put their needs above your need
to "get something."

In public settings, while you are certainly freer to simply gather data and make
assessments, always respect the owners and
always respect the witnesses. Consider that
while most people in such settings may have
no fear, a few might have been affected
adversely by what's going on. Offer them
information and referrals.

Ghost Hunting No Nos

Do not go to any location without full permission of
the owner or leaseholders and the inhabitants. Don't investigate a public location—
restaurant, museum, hotel—without permission. Do not trespass in cemeteries—or any-
place else for that matter. You might get
thrown in jail.

Don't go alone. There are two factors here:
observations and danger. Having other people
with you will provide different viewpoints,
different perceptions, and other sets of eyes
to look for causes of the experiences and
phenomena.

As for danger, there is little the paranormal can do to someone in the physical
world unless one gets clumsy or fearful, or
wants something bad to happen. We have
our own psychic defense mechanisms, and

ghosts or hauntings can't affect us physically. We can still be affected emotionally by the experience, however. Poltergeist phenomena, while physical in nature, have rarely been directed at people other than the agent—who does often harm himself.

Remember that your cases involve living people. While witnesses may seem okay to begin with, sometimes they turn out to be psychologically disturbed. Remember that ghosts don't carry guns and knives, only living people do!

Finally, consider the physical location and potential dangers associated with it. Rats, snakes, rotting timbers, and the like may figure in to some investigations.

Don't jump to conclusions. Always consider all possibilities, normal and paranormal, before coming to your conclusion about what's happening.

Don't believe technology over human perceptions. This may be repetitive, but it's *very* important, given the weighty authority that so many amateur ghost hunting groups attach to technology. Again, you may get something anomalous, but don't jump to the conclusion that a reading or photo relates to a spirit simply because *you* can't think of any other explanation.

Don't scare people with pronouncements of ghosts unless you are sure of what is going on, and they can handle such news. You could be worsening an already bad situation, leaving them to find someone else to help them, and leaving a more psychologically disturbed group for the next investigator.

Don't leave the situation and the people without some kind of resolution or referral for further help. Always give them good information about psychic phenomena.

Don't involve the media without discussing all the ramifications with the people involved at the location. You don't want to be at the center of a media situation that causes your clients more stress.

Don't promise to get rid of the ghost or haunting or poltergeist for sure. You can provide possible resolution, a likely understanding of what's going on, and certainly referrals and information, but *no one* can *guarantee* the removal of paranormal phenomena.

 I hope these Dos and Don'ts are helpful both to potential investigators and to people who may consider bringing in a ghost hunter.

20

BEING PSYCHIC

ONSIDERING THAT PSYCHIC ABILITY is at the center of any model of apparitions and poltergeists as well as hauntings, you might wonder about how to become more psychic or even if doing so is a good idea. Many who do research and investigation in and around psychic phenomena never call themselves psychic and would likely not personally seek out methods of learning to be psychic.

Being psychic and researching psychic abilities of others are distinctly different. Having personal experiences with an apparition or haunting and witnessing poltergeist activity is not a prerequisite to researching haunting and poltergeist phenomena. In fact, some argue that having the abilities can get in the way of conducting research, leading to incorrect assessments of what's going on.

People often ask me if a psychic experience lead me to study parapsychology and are surprised to learn that, aside from an occasional flash of who was on the other end of a ringing phone, I was as

Sometimes psychic Neva Turnock worked on cases with the author.

psychic as a stone. Today that's different because of having been around psychics and active cases, which lead me to notice my own psychic-like experiences.

As I became more involved with parapsychology I paid more attention to my own anomalous experiences and apparent psi-derived information I had. When I have had such experiences I put on my parapsychologist hat and look normal explanations for the events. The more that I have paid attention to my experiences, the more I seem to have.

I have discovered that my own psychic perceptions during an investigation can point me in the right direction for detecting anomalies with technology, or help me to direct the psychics toward a particular place or person. I still play the role of investigator and field researcher by picking apart the data from the witnesses, psychics, and technology. Nonetheless the psychic ability I've developed over the years has definitely been of value to me in my investigations.

EVERYONE HAS PSI ABILITY

PSI IS DISTRIBUTED throughout the entire population. However, some people seem to have greater psychic abilities than others do. Psi is a normal process that we all use—often without awareness. Conscious psychic experiences, while common, occur less frequently than other kinds of experiences. Yet psi is operating all the time just as other senses operate all the time—during awake time, anyway. What we perceive consciously is not everything that our senses receive.

Research has shown that psi is correlated with a variety of factors from variables to emotional moods to belief factors and even environ- mental conditions.

PERSONALITY

ONE OF THE CLEAREST FINDINGS, at least in lab situations, is that extroverts tend to perform better at psi tasks than introverts do. Perhaps extroverts are more willing to verbalize unusual perceptions; or perhaps introverts internalize the input from psi without differentiating it from other perceptions.

People who score higher on an intuitive scale than those who think through things logically tend to show more psi potential. People who have more psychic experiences tend to be more suggestible than those who do not have such experiences. Skeptics point to the suggestibility factor to assert that "they're just imagining things." However, it is more likely that suggestible people may let their minds notice and consider unusual signals, whereas nonsuggestible people may simply dismiss such percep- tions.

CREATIVITY

RESEARCH WITH GROUPS of writers, artists, musicians, and other creative folks has shown that psi is corre- lated with creative ability. Interestingly, psychic and science fiction writers in the mid-20th Century described psychic abilities as talents as similar to musical or artistic talent. Everyone has some degree of creativity and psychic ability, but the amount of talent as well as the ways in which the talents manifest varies from person to person. Some people can draw, others sculpt, others write, and so on. Perhaps creative people, who are open to new ideas and letting their minds go off in unusual directions are simply more likely to notice psychic information as "different."

Belief

THE BELIEF IN THE POSSIBILITY OF PSI seems to provide safe ground for someone to be a bit psychic. Apparently, the belief that psi is a *reality* allows for more noticeable experiences and expressions of psi ability. Believing that psi exists believing and that you are psychic are not the same thing, however. Many people believe in psychics but can't for a moment accept that they, too, are psychic.

To increase your psychic abilities beyond simply noticing what's already there—which is the first step— you must examine your beliefs around those abilities. Consider if you can accept that *you* might *be* psychic. Accepting that you *might* be psychic seems to have less impact than believing that you *can* be psychic or that you actually are psychic. The final step is beyond believing. It is *knowing* that you are psychic and can use the psi perceptual processes you have. Such beliefs can be difficult to incorporate due to the many influences on your belief system from birth.

Culture and Upbringing

Our beliefs are tied to our culture, local society, education, and family upbringing. In cultures where psi is part of the belief system, it appears that there are more psychic experiences in the population. In such a culture, what we call psi experiences may not be described as "paranormal" and the local belief structure may consider such occurrences to be a normal part of human experience. People in cultures that incorporate psi as normal probably consider someone *not* having the experiences as paranormal—or perhaps subnormal.

What our culture believes about the form and magnitude of psi probably shapes the kinds of experiences we have, how frequently we have them and have intense the experiences are. For example, an intense belief in spirits of the ancestors probably has an affect on the number apparitions seen and reported. Basically biases in a culture's belief system shape psi.

Anti-psi sentiments in some religions and certainly in more technological societies can suppress the incidence of psi. In such belief systems, there's little reinforcement for the experiences and little encouragement to discuss them. When one does so, one risks ridicule or being accused of abnormality, and even of being "possessed" by evil forces.

The beliefs of the family unit affect how accepting or rejecting we are of psi. Being brought up in a family that accepts anomalous experiences as normal encourages psi, while the opposite is also true. Educational experience can have an affect on psi experiences, positive or negative. Western culture tends to educate kids out of being psychic, setting limits on them by telling them that the experiences they're having simply can't be real or result from something abnormal.

Earth Energy

DR. MICHAEL PERSINGER investigated how the magnetic field generated by the Earth impacts human beings and their behavior across a number of social sciences. After studying parapsychological literature Persinger looked specifically at correlations between psychic experiences and changes in the local geomagnetic fields. He analyzed lab research and reported spontaneous experiences, from psychic dreams to apparitions, hauntings, and poltergeists. He found such that as the Earth's magnetic field goes up and down, globally and in a given area, people report varying types of psychic experiences.

The findings suggest that experiences of apparitions often take place when the local geomagnetic activity is high, not quiet. This finding is the reason that Persinger's explanation of artificially induced hallucinations seems reasonable, even though the hallucinations lack the interactivity of actual apparitional encounters. Other research suggests a connection between highs in geomagnetic field activity and poltergeist activity and PK in general, as well as a connection between the highs and precognitive experiences.

Clairvoyant and telepathic experiences seem to be correlated to lows in the local geomagnetic field. This is interesting considering that hauntings seem to correlate to unusually high local magnetic fields, on a variety of frequencies besides just the geomagnetic. Perhaps hauntings are fundamentally different from psychic experience, as some have suggested.

THE STARS

WHEN IT COMES TO HAVING A PSYCHIC EXPERIENCE, be it seeing a ghost or having a premonition, an absence of other activity can be key. We tend to notice things when the locale is quiet, with little noise or other activity to distract us, which is probably why people tend to have more ghost sightings at night.

Some studies have suggested that there's a particular window in Local Sidereal Time, or LST, that allows people to be more psychically receptive. Sidereal time is measured not by the rotation of the Earth around its axis or the position of the sun in the sky, but by looking at the particular placement of stars and constellations overhead. The sidereal day is a few minutes shorter than our 24-hour solar day, so LST does not match up directly with normal clock time. That means that a specific time on the sidereal clock shifts from day to day. You can obtain sidereal clock programs for your computer at several Web sites on the Internet.

A window of about an hour around 13:30 LST seems to correlate to an upswing in psi experiences. Research shows that during this window, people in psi experiments score higher on the tasks than at other times of day or night. Perhaps something in the sky with a fixed position with respect to the Earth affects psi functioning. Another possibility is that psi functioning is influenced by some emission from the opposite direction, which is at least partially blocked by the Earth. The signal, generally coming from the center of the galaxy inhibits anomalous cognition, as the Earth blocks the inhibitor signal for the hour around 13:30, the effect increases.

As it happens, the LST correlation seems to support the tagging of ESP as receptive psi, since the rise in effect is based on the *receiver's* Local Sidereal Time, even when the *sender* is thousands of miles away. There hasn't been a real attempt to correlate LST to hauntings and apparition cases as yet, but that should be coming.

21

DEVELOPING PSI

O TO ANY BOOKSTORE to the metaphysics section and you'll find dozens of books on psychic development. The techniques vary dramatically, from meditation to changing one's daily diet. Many recommend following a particular spiritual path; others—very few, unfortunately—recommend staying grounded in reality. It seems that any one psychic development book or course may help a few people, but no technique seems to be universal. Who is right can be difficult to assess, as it's almost impossible to know if the author is actually psychic, and capable of picking out what techniques and exercises can work for a wide spectrum of people as opposed to those things that worked for the author.

Since there are so many psychological and environmental influences on psi, it may be that the method that worked for the author doesn't work for anyone else. We are all different, and while there are commonalities, some things work for some people but rarely for everyone. But there are some techniques that do appear to work for everyone.

NOTICE YOUR EXPERIENCES

PSYCHIC Alex Tanous once told me that if people
would simply open their eyes and take conscious
note of the world around them, they'd see a lot
more to it. We tend to filter out so much of what
goes in our normal senses, simply not noticing large
amounts of what comes into our perceptions. It's
no surprise that we simply don't notice the psychic
input. This makes even more sense when one
considers that most psi-received information seems to
be related to mundane things rather than dramatic
events.

One of the simplest tech-
niques is to be con-
sciously aware of
your surround-
ings and
how
you

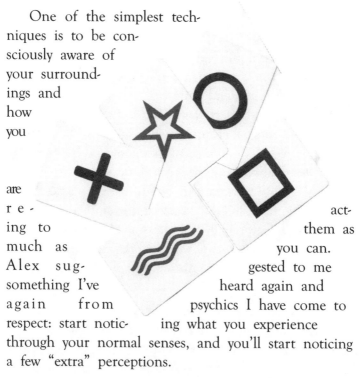

are
r e -   acting to   them as
much as   you can.
Alex sug-   gested to me
something I've   heard again and
again   from   psychics I have come to
respect: start notic-   ing what you experience
through your normal senses, and you'll start noticing
a few "extra" perceptions.

Here's a popular technique for increasing your psi ability. Spend a few minutes each day consciously noticing what you are perceiving with each of your senses. Take a moment and really look around with your eyes. Don't just scan the environment. Make a conscious effort to be aware of everything your eyes see.

Move on to your hearing. Don't simply note the louder noises around you. Take conscious note of the background noises, the sounds outside the room, and even the building that you might be in. The creaking sounds the chair is making, or the rustling of the fabric of your clothing. Notice your breathing, and any other bodily sounds.

Move on to smell, touch, and even taste. For touch, don't limit yourself to your fingers and hands. Notice how the fabric of your clothing, your shoes, watchband, and glasses all feel. Consider pressure, temperature, and even pain perceptions. For taste, notice how your mouth tastes, and add in some foods or drink to exercise the sense. Do the same with smell.

After a time you will likely begin to notice a few "other" perceptions and things popping into your head. You'll notice sensations and information you can't connect to your five senses. Take special notice of these, as they are likely representative of your psi-related perceptions. The more you notice these perceptions, the more you *will* notice.

Sense the relationship of things and people around you to your moods and physical feelings. If you are having psychic experiences, keep track of how you are feeling, physically, mentally, and emotionally, before, during, and after the experience. Note what you've eaten, and whether there are any unusual situations going on in your life, any concerns, stresses, or other interpersonal reactions. If there are, *write them down*—or use a tape recorder to keep track. Keep a journal.

By observing your personal circumstances and feelings while having psychic experiences, you can look for patterns that may lead to or cause the experiences. You may then be able to narrow down what allows you to be psychic, and devise some exercise to repeat the experiences. The more you learn about why you have your experiences, the more you may be able to control their appearance and direct the abilities. If you are not having such experiences, this exercise may not only help your powers

The author in Australia with psychic Aiko Gibo and an aboriginal musician.

of observation, it may also allow you to notice experience that you had not considered psychic before. However, don't go overboard in labeling things "paranormal," since you may end up misleading yourself about how truly psychic you are, which can cause some problems.

There's also the flip side here: the above exercise is a good way to actually get rid of unwanted psychic experience. By seeing the patterns in your life that cause the experiences, you can also learn what you need to do to avoid them.

EXERCISE YOUR PSI

ACTIVELY EXERCISE YOUR ABILITIES. There are several books on remote viewing that include exercises and experiments you might try. One interesting exercise I've found to work well will require someone else's help.

Have a friend or loved one gather various objects of different shapes, colors, and use or purpose. Everything from a baseball to a violin, from a superhero action figure to a roll of toilet paper is workable here. These items should not be shown to you.

Have your helper select one of the objects as the "target," and place it in a box on a table. Have her really focus on the object, and even visualize it glowing. Next, have your helper then take three or four other items— these should all be as different from one another as possible—and place them in boxes on a table. The

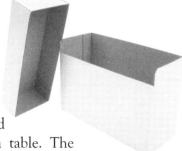

boxes should be the same size, closed, and there should be no way to see within them.

With your helper facing away from the table but still focusing on the object—what it is, not necessarily where it is—come into the room, approach the table, and look over the boxes. Move from box to box, perhaps using your hands above them as a guide. Sense if one of the items is different from the others. It may feel warmer or cooler or different in some other way.

Make a first and second choice of which box contains the object. Then remove the objects from the boxes and note which item was in your first choice box. Have your helper state out loud what the chosen item was, then turn around. Let your helper know whether you were right or wrong.

The next step is to sense what the object actually is before taking it out of the box. In other words, once you've chosen which box you believe has the target, ask yourself what the item might look like, feel like, smell like, and be used for.

Out loud, describe *anything* that comes into mind, talking about shape, size, texture, and any feelings you have about the item and its uses. But do *not* try to immediately figure out what it is.

In other words, don't name it "a banana" or "a Superman action figure." From past research, it's become clear that as soon as a subject names a thing, the mind begins to fill in any missing imagery about it. A bright red ball becomes an apple, for example.

As a next step, describe any imagery or perceptions for any of the items, even while deciding which is the actual target. You may find you are better at determining information about the objects, but not which one is the helper's choice.

In General

IF YOU HOPE TO PURSUE PSYCHIC DEVELOPMENT, make sure you use common sense above all else. If something you read or hear makes no sense to you, don't force it. As I mentioned, different techniques work for different people. Don't make any drastic dietary or nutritional changes in your life-style simply because the "teacher" says it worked for him—at least not without first checking with a doctor. Psychic development need not be tied to any particular spiritual or religious practice. The evidence of this is that people in just about every culture and religion have exhibited psychic abilities and experiences.

If you have any dramatic increase in psychic experiences, especially ones that cause you stress or other concerns, back off from what you're doing. Take the time to review your progress and the experiences themselves, as would a researcher looking at the experiences from the outside. Look not only for the patterns that give rise to psi in the first place, but also for those that seem tied to the experiences you personally consider negative.

STAY GROUNDED IN THE REAL WORLD.
IT IS WHERE WE LIVE.

INDEX

A

adolescents 103
agent 103
Altea, Rosemary 39
American Association for the
        Advancement of Scienc 49
American Society for Psychical
        Research (ASPR) 43, 140, 154
Anderson, George 39
anomalous cognition 8, 20
apparitional PK 77, 111
apparitions 34, 61-66, 76, 116, 118,
        120, 123, 134
Ashley's Restaurant 148, 150
astral body 35, 71
automatic writing 40

B

Bannister, Roger 25
Banta Inn 109, 110
belief 53, 108, 173
Bird Cage Theater 86
Blue Lady 63, 68, 72, 79
Borland, Joan 110
Brookdale Lodge 90, 153
Browne, Sylvia 39
Brugger, Peter 125

C

Café Van Kleef, ghost of 38
Caidin, Martin 24, 26, 148
clairvoyance 19, 52, 118, 175
communication 37, 69
Conan-Doyle, Sir Arthur 42
Coover, John 47
Cornell, A. D. (Tony) 111
Crandon, Mina 45
creativity 172
crisis apparition 65
culture 17, 174

D

Dalton, Kathy 56
deathbed apparitions 65
decline effect 51
deja vu 92
discarnate entity 13, 120
dowsing 21
duration 87, 102, 115

E

Edward, John 39
emotion 11, 83, 100
environment 91
ESP cards 45-46
expectations 17
expressive psi 9
extended sensory perception 8, 15

F

FFytche, Dominic 126
Foundation for Research on the
        Nature of Man 47
Fox sisters 42
fraud 38, 106

G

Garrett, Eileen 48, 117
Gasparetto, Luis 40
Gauld, Alan 111
Gauld Cornell Criteria 112
Geller, Uri 29
geomagnetic field 124
ghost 12, 71, 74, 79, 85, 118-
        119, 135, 151, 155
ghost hunters 72, 106, 161, 200
ghost hunting 163-167
ghosts 9, 60, 66, 69-70, 76, 125, 199
Gibo, Aiko 19, 21, 56, 113, 181
Global Consciousness Project (GCP)
        58
God-Speed luncheon 43

H

hallucinations 75, 95-96, 114, 119,
        123
Harary, Keith 8
haunting RSPK 97
hauntings 10, 65, 81, 97, 123,
healing 27, 180
holographic haunting 118, 120
Houck, Jack 30
Houdini, Harry 45
Hugo, Victor 40
Human Energy Systems Laboratory
        58
human machine interactions 31

I

imprint 90
intention 24, 25
interactive hallucinations 12, 119

J

James, William 43

L

Leyser, Kip 133
living agent 11
Local Sidereal Time 176
low frequency sounds 127, 159

M

macro-PK effects 55
magnetic 93, 122
magnetometers 93, 94
Manganelli, Dave 124
Margery 44
Martin, Annette 38, 63, 72, 79

McDougall, William 44, 45
mediums 37-39, 43, 47, 117
metal bending 29
micro-PK effects 55
Monroe, Robert 35
Moss Beach Distillery 61, 63, 64, 68
Murray, Stache Margaret 121
Myles, Suzane 21

N

near death experiences NDE 35,
    36, 95, 125
Newcomb, Simon 43
Nichols, Andrew 124
noisy ghost 11, 27, 99

O

old hag" phenomenon 128
Ouija Board 37
out-of-the-body OBE 34, 35 66, 125

P

Parapsychological Association 50, 163
parapsychologists 16, 28, 49, 54,
    97, 122, 130, 148, 163
parapsychology 7, 8, 13, 41, 50, 200
Parapsychology Foundation
    48, 117, 163
past life memories 93
perception 17, 71, 85, 92
Persinger, Michael 94, 122, 129, 175
personality 172
phantoms 125-128
PK 77, 109
place memory 81
poltergeist 11, 26, 99, 107, 111, 146
postmortem apparitions 64
precognition 22
Prest , Jude Gerard 26
Princeton Engineering Anomalies
    Research (PEAR) la 49
proof 34, 51, 199
psi 7, 13, 71, 73, 76, 89, 94, 107,
    117, 122, 173, 182
psi ability univeral 171
psi activity & unseen agent 112
psi missing 46, 52
psychic 8, 163, 170, 180
psychic development 180, 184
psychic surgery 27, 28
psychokinesis 9, 23, 87
psychometry 20,-21, 81, 89

R

radiesthesia 21
reading 18, 20, 81
receptive psi 8
recording mechanism 72, 96
recordings as hauntings 11
recurrent spontaneous psychokinesis
    27, 77, 100
remote viewing 20, 54, 56

repetition 82
responsibility 110
retrocognition 22, 92
Rhine, J.B. & Louisa 45, 46, 53
Rhine, Joseph Banks 44, 51, 52
Rhine Research Center 47, 163
Rix, Joanna 133
Roberts, Jane 40
Rogers, Bob 119
Roll, William G. 27, 99, 100, 124
RSPK 27, 105
RSPK agent 150

S

Schmeidler, Gertrude 48, 53
Schwartz, Gary 58
self healing 28
senses 16
Seth Material 40
setting 102
sheep-goat effect 48, 53
skeptics 95, 129
sleep paralysis 129
Society for Psychical Research (SPR)
    7, 41
Spiritualism church 42, 48
spontaneous psychokinetic activity 7,
    66, 113
SPR 163
staring 57
stresses 11, 100, 105, 148, 150
Survival 9, 33
symbolism 104
T
Tandy, Vic 126
Tanous, Alex 179
Tart, Charles 77
telekinesis 26
telepathy 18, 52, 74, 118, 175
Tombstone 84, 86
Turnock, Neva 171
Tyrrell, G. N. M. 64

U

unexplained knowing 8
unseen agency 112
USS Hornet 118, 119, 120, 121

V

Van Praagh, James 39
W
Warcollier, Rene 47
water 151
water-witching 21
Weiss, Brian 36

Z

Zener, Karl 45

PROFESSOR PARANORMAL

LOYD AUERBACH is a mentalist and psychic entertainer. He is also the Director of the Office of Paranormal Investigations, a consulting Editor and columnist for FATE Magazine, a professor at JFK University and President of the Psychic Entertainers Association, a past President of the California Society for Psychic Study, and co-founder of the Paranormal Research Organization (paranormal-research.org), which is aimed at networking and bringing professional standards to paranormal investigators. He holds a masters in parapsychology and has been investigating the Paranormal for over 25 years. Loyd Auerbach is an international expert on ghosts, poltergeists and psychic experience.

Visit Professor Paranormal s website at mindreader.com or contact him via email at esper@california.com or by phone at the Office of Paranormal Investigations, 415-249-9275.